The Prosecutor
Trial Judge
The Trial of the Future: Challenge to the Law (*with Murray Gordon*)

OUR CITIES BURN

WHILE WE PLAY COPS AND ROBBERS

Bernard Botein

SIMON AND SCHUSTER · NEW YORK

To Marian

Published by Simon and Schuster
Rockefeller Center, 630 Fifth Avenue
New York, New York 10020

First printing

SBN 671-21269-9
Library of Congress Catalog Card Number: 72-80618
Designed by Edith Fowler
Manufactured in the United States of America
by H. Wolff Book Mfg. Co., Inc.

ACKNOWLEDGMENTS

I have been associated with the administration of criminal justice for well over a generation—as prosecutor, defense counsel, Presiding Justice of one of the two State Supreme Court Appellate Divisions which administer the courts of New York City, and more recently as associate chairman of that city's Criminal Justice Coordinating Council.

In these last two capacities, I seemed to be wrestling with a crisis a day, mostly due to lack of funds and resources. At times we felt we were holding the courts together, particularly the criminal terms, with Scotch Tape and safety pins. We planned and plotted to wheedle appropriations from the budget authorities for more facilities and personnel; and we were too busy grappling with the grim world as it is to daydream about a world as it should be—a world with no slums, no ignorance, unemployment or other evils which we believe breed crime.

This book originated in the nineteenth Thomas M. Cooley Lectures, a series of five lectures I delivered at the University of Michigan Law School in the autumn of 1970. I spoke in a pragmatic vein, trying to present a balance of the short-range reform possibilities with the long-range aspirations. Dean Francis Allen of the law school, who invited me to deliver the lectures, has encouraged me to expand them into a book in the hope of attracting a larger audience. I am most grateful for his wise counsel and co-operation.

I am greatly in debt to Gerald Stern, who in his capacity as deputy director of administration of the courts in the First Judicial Department of New York State had worked closely with me when I was Presiding Justice. I turned to him for assistance first in preparing the Cooley Lectures and later in welding them into this book; and his assistance has been invaluable. He is one of the most knowledgeable men in America on the practice and the theory of the administration of criminal justice, and he always seemed to have at hand a fund of marvelous material to buttress every point I wished to make.

Finally, it was as always comforting to have my law associate, Arthur Kramer, with his impeccable taste and logic, read and criticize every draft of the book.

CONTENTS

INTRODUCTION

The American public still regards its crime problem as a game of cops and robbers. If the police are diligent, efficient and honest, identify and arrest most wrongdoers, are not hamstrung by liberal court decisions, crime will be checked and disappear from our streets. In the minds of the people, and unfortunately of many government officials, it is as simple as all that. But there are no simple solutions to the crime problem.

Few give thought to what happens after the arrest. The suspect must be arraigned, afforded reasonable bail, prosecuted and defended; if convicted, he must be sentenced, released on either probation or suspended sentence or sent to prison and later possibly paroled. If any of these processes fail or falter, the effectiveness of the police function may be frustrated. In fact, none of these components of the criminal-justice system will operate with optimum efficiency unless all mesh on a productive level.

Too many of us, however, believe that the police offer the full and final answer to crime in the streets. That notion is nourished by the books we read and the television programs we view. In Dodge City each week, in a nineteenth-century setting, Marshal Dillon more often than not shoots it out and kills the outlaw. This is the neatest way to dispense criminal justice—no precious presumption of innocence, no indictment, trial, judicial agonizing in the sentencing decision, no corrections or parole challenges, and no prospect that the prisoner will return to society a more embittered and reckless criminal.

Communications media seldom portray the conditions which are most troublesome to the authorities. The story usually ends with the arrest of the culprit. The viewer or reader is not told how many festering months or years the defendant spent in detention prison awaiting trial because of court calendar congestion; nor is he told how prolonged incarceration contributes to the overcrowding and the unspeakable conditions which breed hatred of society among the inmates, guilty and innocent alike—and incite prison riots. Only on the relatively rare occasions when a prison outbreak occurs or a Jimmy Hoffa applies for relief on parole does the public become aware that there is more to the crime problem than the arrest process, that there is a vast administrative machinery which moves into operation after arrest.

If in a past generation crime became rampant west of the Pecos, good citizens opined that the way to curb it was to hire more law-enforcement officers to bring in more outlaws, dead or alive. I am afraid our thinking today is no more sophisticated than the frontier thinking of a century ago. If the crime rate escalates, hire more police to detect and arrest more offenders. Never a thought to whether jails already overcrowded can accommodate the increased population; whether already understaffed prosecutors and public defenders, probation and parole agencies, can physically—not to mention adequately—handle any more cases; whether court delays, already intolerable in most cities, will become so pervasive as to make a mockery of the entire administration of criminal justice.

This frantic, panicky pouring of more resources into police agencies—the maw of the criminal-justice system—this preoccupation with ingestion rather than digestion, is reminiscent of the famed pelican whose beak holds more than his belly can. It is as irresponsible, thoughtless and mischievous as the overfeeding of babies to stop them from crying.

I do not quarrel with the need to strengthen the police—through modern equipment and management methods as well as additional manpower. Such newly added resources, however, will be largely wasted, could indeed create so heavy a backwash of unprocessed cases that all police work would degenerate, unless the other agencies in the criminal-justice system are strengthened proportionately so that they can handle efficiently the burden of new business thrust upon them. This is not likely to happen so long as the national audience loses all interest in the play after the first dramatic act of arrest. More prosecutors and defense counsel are needed, more courtrooms, judges and a wide range of nonjudicial personnel to keep pace with the unremitting surge of business funneled into the courts by the police.

The probation and correctional processes must be buttressed, if we are to place any reliance on the rehabilitative function of the system. Probation and parole officers are too overburdened with huge caseloads to be of much assistance to convicted offenders.

Public indifference also serves to perpetuate an ever-growing permanent criminal population. The police force is out of balance with the agencies, such as probation, corrections and parole, which, adequately resourced, can reclaim some criminals to useful lives.

The criminal-justice system requires enormous additional funding to function effectively. In preparing budgets, with demands from so many competing government units, officials empowered to allocate funds are influenced importantly by their own awareness of an agency's needs, and also by the political clout the agency can assert. The muscle for political clout is usually the force of public opinion, to which officeholders are always responsive. The public as well as most officeholders believe the police are the complete answer to the crime problem. The other agencies so essential to the administration of criminal justice enjoy no such recognition and therefore lag far behind the police in securing adequate budgetary appropriations. This is one of the areas in which the ignorance of public and government undermines the entire criminal-justice system.

As I am about to turn the manuscript of this book over to the publisher, the nation is horror-stricken at the shocking news of the killing of forty-two guards and inmates in Attica Prison. During the agonizing days of negotiation between the prisoners and the authorities, the latter agreed to comply with most of the demands made by the leaders of the uprising for betterment of prison conditions. These were mostly measures that penologists and advocates of prison reform had been urging for generations. I have no doubt that the deplorable conditions of prison life and the foot dragging of prison reform were important elements in this disaster. It is a melancholy commentary that had such reforms been instituted earlier the outbreak would not have occurred; and that the aftermath of this tragedy will be that New York State and other jurisdictions will now pour resources into their correction systems which they have consistently refused before.

Ignorance coupled with a sense of impotence frequently leads to vengeful and fretful expressions. A 1966 survey by the National Opinion Research Center in Washington, D.C., asked citizens what they thought were the most important steps that could be taken to reduce crime in their city. They were given three choices: (1) repressive measures, (2) ameliorating social conditions, or (3) strengthening morals. Sixty percent recommended repressive measures, tougher police action and "cracking down on teenagers." Most respondents said that sentences were too lenient.[1] A 1965 nationwide Gallup Poll also found that a majority of persons interviewed believed that the courts are too lenient with defendants. Only two percent responded that the courts were too harsh. Yet, many of the most experienced and profound students of our criminal-justice system believe that statutory sentences in America are much too harsh—far more so than in Europe. Polls such as this one, reflecting a dismal ignorance of the functioning of the criminal-justice system, nevertheless influence the actions of public officials in the executive, legislative and judicial branches, who themselves often know little more than their constituency about the complex field of penology.

Even the imperturbable British, usually so complacent about the caliber of their law enforcement, have begun to show signs of irritability. A few months ago two high-ranking Scotland Yard officials urged "no more parole or suspended sentences for men convicted of crimes of violence." They also said, "There must be penal establishments for them where there will be more discipline, more work, where they will perform tasks in their cells, and there will be no television, no radio, no choice of food, no weekend leave." The senior official added, "I will not go so far as to say that they should be beaten, but one should see to it that they got it into their minds that they did not want to come back." [2]

One way of releasing substantial resources to deal with serious crimes is to take a long, hard look at our penal laws with a view to redefining criminal conduct. Should not public drunkenness, which accounts for one third of the arrests in this country, be removed from the criminal lexicon; and are not the civil authorities better qualified than the criminal courts to treat with the social and medical problems presented by the chronic police-case alcoholic? Should not all except the most serious traffic and housing violations be channeled to administrative agencies? Too many insignificant categories of criminal conduct, such as the heinous crime of peddling without a license, clutter our courts. It is paradoxical that large numbers of hardened and serious offenders slip through the criminal-justice system because of its lack of resources, while so much of the meager resources available is squandered on petty matters.

The owner of a general store in a small town would be appalled at the antiquated management and record-keeping techniques employed by most of the criminal-justice agencies. Slow, tortuous and expensively repetitive entries are made in record books manually by high-salaried employees who could pose as models for the stereotypes of nineteenth-century bookkeepers sitting on high stools and poring over bulky ledgers. The agencies should be able to hire management consultant firms to devise better ways of doing business and should have the funds to employ professional administrators assisted by a wide range of trained management skills.

Two factors contribute to the persistence of these wasteful procedures. One is an analogue of the resistance offered by trade unions to labor-saving techniques that would lead to a reduction in the work force. (Most government units, at least in the large cities, are fully or significantly unionized.) In addition, the sensitivity of management in government organizations to economy measures is not honed sharp by the inexorable balance sheets and profit and loss statements which, if unfavorable, could unseat management itself in a business firm.

Second, the initial installation of control and efficiency programs is quite costly, although once installed they will generally prove productive of great savings. It is difficult to squeeze large sums of money, even for capital expenditures, out of pinched local government budgets.

Compounding the weaknesses of the individual agencies of criminal justice is their failure to function truly as a system. Although critically interdependent, each functions as an island unto itself. They compete for funds and set their separate goals independently of the other agencies.

Criminal-justice personnel in all the units must learn that they have many problems in common; and that even those problems peculiar to individual agencies can be handled better by working more closely with the others. A particular agency in need would stand a better chance of securing additional resources if it were supported by a network of agencies. If a police department wants its men on the streets and not frittering away their time waiting for their cases to be reached in court, it must support modernization of the courts. On the other hand, if the courts want their large volume of warrants served promptly and efficiently by the police, they must support the police department's thrust for more manpower and a modernized administrative structure for the service of court warrants. Again, if the courts want better service from prosecutors, public defenders and probation officers, upon whom they are so dependent, they must support appropriate funding for these agencies.

Each agency, instead of competing as it now does for available funds, should have a voice in how local, state and federal crime control funds are apportioned for all agencies. The importance of a single planning agency, representing all parts of the system, is underscored by the present availability of large amounts of federal funds for use by localities to help control crime.

The National Crime Commission (the President's Commission on Law Enforcement and the Administration of Justice) underlined in its 1967 report the need to construct "formal machinery for planning" on every state and local level.[3] It urged that the first step in what it called a "national strategy" to control crime should be comprehensive planning by a single body in each jurisdiction, composed of representatives of all criminal-justice agencies. The Commission viewed concerted and systematic planning as a necessary prelude, as well as a spur, to action.

Too few cities, however, have perceived the advantage of having comprehensive planning agencies. In New York City, Mayor John V. Lindsay formed the Criminal Justice Coordinating Council, composed of private citizens and representatives of all public and private agencies playing any significant role in the administration of criminal justice. The Council apportions federal crime-control funds among the various criminal-justice agencies in the city. The Council and its staff work closely with all segments of the system, attempting both to resolve problems which arise and to encourage the development of new programs which can be funded under the federal Safe Streets Act. Indicative of the scope of its powers and functions, the Council has announced recently that because of the past funding imbalance, most of the federal funds made available in the immediate future would be directed at curing court and correctional inadequacies.

Money itself—even lots of it—will not necessarily assure sensible reforms in the administration of criminal justice. Resistance to change, so chronic in most government circles, must be overcome. Innovation must be encouraged and the attitudes of those within the system must be sufficiently flexible to permit and accommodate to change.

Better personnel selection methods should be developed by the various agencies. In this connection, the selection of judges should be removed from politics. The public has a low estimate of the persons who man the criminal-justice system—an opinion which has soured into deep resentment among certain ethnic and low-income groups which encounter the law with some frequency. Officials administering criminal justice cannot dismiss this brooding, dangerous anger by pointing to the massive workloads they unquestionably carry.

But, of course, money is an indispensable element to improve the administration of criminal justice and to eliminate some root causes we have every reason to believe foster crime. The large amounts needed cannot realistically be found at the municipal level. Only the federal government presently has the means to make this available. Federal grants to local crime-control efforts to date have been too small to make any noticeable difference. A total of $480 million allocated for fiscal year 1971, spread out over fifty states, just does not go very far. Many times that amount will have to be distributed to bring the criminal-justice system to a fair level of effectiveness. And, even so strengthened, it will perform only a holding action until this nation accepts and meets such challenges as intolerance, bad housing, unemployment, inadequate job training and other conditions which make men desperate and bitter toward their society. This book, however, is limited largely to dealing with conditions after the fact of crime—with the operation of the criminal-justice system.

PART ONE

REDEFINITIONS

I OUR SYSTEM OF CRIMINAL JUSTICE: SOME INITIAL OBSERVATIONS

Serious crime has reached alarming new heights in this country. According to the National Commission on the Causes and Prevention of Violence, every resident of a metropolitan area stands a chance of one in 125 each year of becoming a victim of homicide, rape, assault or robbery. Projecting these figures over the course of a lifetime, many Americans face an almost even chance of being the victim of a serious crime; in some cities, and in certain sections of most cities, the odds are considerably shorter. Another recent study showed that the danger of becoming subject to violent crime is fifty times greater in some sections of New York City than in other neighborhoods in the same city.[1] What these statistics mean is that in many areas (and especially in the slums) people cannot walk the streets without running a very real risk of being mugged; burglaries of apartments, holdups of retail stores, and experimenting with hard drugs by children eleven and twelve years of age are common occurrences.

In all parts of the country, in cities and suburban areas alike, the fear of violent crime continues to mount. Not only is it constantly voiced, but significant changes in life styles are to be seen as people have adjusted to new ways of life to avoid exposure to crime. While excesses in caution are certain to occur, this manifest fear cannot be dismissed as unfounded hysteria. City residents are afraid to walk the streets at night; they are afraid to enter their self-service elevators or to venture into the basements of their buildings. They install multiple locks on their doors and windows, and recent reports indicate that sales of burglar alarms, whistles and household weapons are reaching new peaks. As one small reflection of this problem, it has been pointed out recently that New York's theater attendance has decreased as a result of the widespread fear of strolling at night into Manhattan's famous Great White Way. Owners of stores have complained about the steadily declining volume of business after dark.

Perhaps most disturbing of all is that the fear of violence is causing more and more citizens to take drastic steps to achieve a degree of protection they feel the police cannot provide. In Virginia, a suburban homeowner recently shot his paper boy after hearing a suspicious noise outside his home. In some parts of California and in other areas judges are presiding in court with guns under their robes.

Shopkeepers by the thousands in many parts of the country are selling their wares and giving change from their cash registers with guns tucked under their aprons. A gun-toting storeowner who had been held up several times told the story recently, in *Newsweek* magazine, of a customer who entered his store and stood briefly with his back to the counter. The customer reached into his coat and turned around, and the storeowner, in fear of another holdup, pulled out a gun and was about to shoot. The customer held a small puppy in his hand. The storeowner "sighed heavily, in wonder at what is become of him and his world," *Newsweek* reported. "A puppy," he mused. "I would have shot him." [2] A most graphic manifestation of the infection of fear was reported recently in the New York *Times,* commenting on the high incidence of shootings in Detroit. "In an East Side grocery store," reported the *Times,* "in view of everyone, a clerk sits in a loft with a rifle trained on customers below." [3]

Pervasive fear is only one of the heavy "costs" of crime—the others being serious bodily injuries, mental anguish and losses of money and property—compelling a reexamination of the nation's response to this problem. We can no longer afford to cling to the shibboleths of the past or to assume that timeworn approaches are valid merely because they have survived. Suggesting reforms in a vacuum will have little significance unless we are sufficiently motivated to innovate, to experiment, and to spend larger portions of our gross national income in curbing crime. One practical question at the heart of reform is: What are we willing to pay for effective and durable control of crime so that we may regain the basic freedom we see imperiled?

During the fall of 1970 I gave the annual Thomas M. Cooley series of lectures at the University of Michigan Law School. In spite of the fact that a comprehensive report by the National Crime Commission (the President's Commission on Law Enforcement and the Administration of Justice) had been rendered just three years earlier, I chose for the lectures a subject which has always been a deep concern of mine. Although the Commission had performed a very valuable service by its excellent and sweeping study of crime, I felt that there were aspects of this urgent problem that were still in need of further illumination. I felt also that even a modest but updated presentation could make a contribution, in the context of the digestive period following the Commission's report, by going beyond some of the positions taken by the Commission; and by placing greater emphasis than the Commission did on various corrective steps which should be taken.

The focus of this offering of the lectures in book form will be on what I believe is a rational response to crime through our criminal laws and the agencies which have been given various responsibilities to prevent crime and to apprehend, identify and rehabilitate criminals. The absence here of any prolonged discussion about the relationship of poverty and crime is of course not intended to depreciate the importance of eliminating the morbid and destructive conditions of poverty which are surely associated with much of the serious crime problem troubling this country today.

Although it is clear that a disproportionate number of street crimes are committed by poor people, we have developed no substantial body of information on the causes of crime. Hence we depend largely on what are known as our criminal-justice systems—police, courts, prosecutors, defense attorneys and the personnel of penal institutions and probation and parole agencies—to control criminal behavior. While efforts to improve the living standards of the poor have been made during the past few years, they do not approach the kind of comprehensive attack on poverty which must be made both for the sake of human decency and for the long-range purpose of stemming the tide of rising crime rates.

Relatively little has been done to combat factors such as poverty and narcotics addiction, which seem to be causally related to crime. Abominable living conditions in overcrowded and substandard housing, lack of suitable employment, loss of identity and self-respect, and the intense anger and hopelessness which abound in slum areas are all matters relevant to the prevention of crime. The only effective prescription for our crime problem is also the only effective prescription for a democracy with a decent regard for the dignity and well-being of all its citizens. The prescription embraces, among other ingredients, vastly improved housing, education, job training, job opportunities and social services—long-range goals that government should begin implementing at once both on their own merits and as part of an overall plan to control crime. Such a program could be commenced only after long-range planning, and campaigning against any resistance. This book will be addressed to the more limited, the more immediate and what many would consider the more feasible program of increasing the effectiveness of our criminal-justice system by reforms within that system itself.

Over the short run we should look to a vastly improved system which can expeditiously and fairly identify serious offenders and rehabilitate them while deterring others from engaging in similar conduct. The available evidence indicates that at present we perform none of these functions with any degree of efficiency. High recidivism rates attest, in part, to the failure of the system. Those brought within the correctional process are not corrected. Many more offenders, in fact, are not even apprehended. Only half of all serious crimes are ever reported to the police and of the half that are reported only twenty to twenty-two percent are "cleared" by arrests or confessions. Thus, in only one of every ten serious crimes is anyone even identified by the police as the perpetrator. And because not all of those arrested are subsequently convicted, perhaps one of every fifteen or twenty serious crimes is truly cleared.

Crime in the streets has been termed the country's leading domestic political issue. State and federal officials, conscious of the nation's concern, have shown some awareness recently that revenue-starved municipalities just do not have available a fair fraction of the needed resources to improve their police, courts, and correctional agencies. Until recently they appeared to regard crime as simply another local problem, like garbage collection or potholes in the streets. We have as yet heard little more than rhetoric and received only pitifully inadequate grants from federal and state governments.

Politicians (and every elected public official is a politician, even if motivated solely by the honest and sometimes justified belief that the welfare of his constituency hangs upon his reelection) are niggardly about doling out funds for the criminal-justice system. Consequently, the agencies involved in the administration of criminal justice, with the possible exception of the police, are notoriously budget-starved. They are the stepchildren of the city fathers, and of state and federal governments as well. Perhaps if taxpayers in these cities realized how many of the little-known elements of the criminal-justice process contributed to the failure to control crime, they would be more tolerant of the huge budget required to cope efficiently with crime; and they might even nudge the lawgivers into furnishing law-enforcement agencies with adequate resources.

Of course, all public officeholders and office seekers, in their own individual ways, endorse the nation's war on crime. Attempts to control crime have focused almost entirely on improving police capabilities to detect and apprehend criminals. Over the past few years, campaign platforms of law-and-order candidates have promised an end to the "handcuffing" of police and have urged the broad expansion of police powers. Local and state legislatures, in reaction to the pressure from concerned constituencies, have begun giving the police a greater priority in the allocation of public funds, and some of these funds have been directed toward introducing modern technological advances into the law enforcement process. Spearheading this effort, the federal government has begun giving money to communities for new equipment and approaches not readily available to the police in the past.

While the impact of this new effort to improve police efficiency cannot yet be accurately measured, inevitably many more defendants will be funneled through the criminal-justice system. Placing more, better-trained, and better-equipped police officers on the streets may be necessary, but it results in more arrests, which in turn increase caseloads in the courts to the choking point. When court conditions reach crisis proportions, a few more judges may be added, but they cannot function adequately without more prosecutors, public defenders and probation and parole officers to process the additional court business efficiently. And meanwhile detention jails burst their seams, and we witness riots such as those which raged in 1970 in New York City by defendants detained for long periods of time prior to trial.

The theme of this book is that these criminal-justice agencies are unable to handle properly the increasing volume of cases being thrust upon them. Most criminal-justice agencies are not functioning adequately; they lack the means and the technical expertise to cope with their overwhelming workloads. Their resources are spread so thin that they are unable to devote adequate attention to serious offenders. These inadequacies are compounded by the treatment of the agencies as isolated fragments instead of interlocking parts of an integrated criminal-justice system.

New priorities must be set for the system as a whole if an intelligent attack on crime is to be made and if the system is to function as efficiently and fairly as it should. Consideration must be given to improving the entire system and not merely its initial phase. An arrest is a temporary crime-control mechanism. It removes a suspect from the streets for a period of a few hours before he proceeds to the next stage of this system. It may be the most dramatic and most newsworthy feature of the system, but by no means is it the only important one.

What is "crime"? Since one of every three arrests in this country is for nondisorderly public intoxication, it stands to reason that one major form of crime is a Skid Row drunk sleeping in a doorway or begging for handouts. Other forms of crime are a heated argument in the street, an uncovered garbage can, the possession of an obscene photograph, the smoking of a marijuana cigarette, and murder. Laws defining criminal behavior protect us against ourselves by proscribing what may be dangerous to our health or to our morals; they protect us as well against the harmful acts of others.

Our inability to develop a consistent rationale for what should be deemed criminal is reflected in a variety of inconsistencies. Smoking a marijuana cigarette is punishable by a term in jail, but the harmful habit of chain-smoking cigarettes is perfectly legal. Similar inconsistencies appear in the enforcement of law. Middle-class people who are drunk in public are escorted home or placed in taxicabs while their homeless, impoverished counterparts who reside on Skid Row are often arrested. Sexual activity between consenting adults is regulated by the criminal law, but few who violate the law are punished. In New York City, where adultery has been almost daily acknowledged in open court in divorce cases, there have been virtually no adultery prosecutions.

Even the most cursory assessment of crime suggests that it embraces many different kinds of human conduct and requires many different kinds of approaches. Some crimes we fear, others pose no threat at all. Indeed, some crime is committed by large segments of the population—by the same people who have reason to fear walking in the streets at night or leaving their doors unlocked.

What all this means is that we probably have not done a very good job of defining what conduct should be criminal. When we consider in addition that the agencies of criminal justice are overwhelmed with work, it is even more obvious that too much reliance has been placed on the criminal law. The system has been unable to prevent the repetition of crimes by the same offenders—more than half of the people released from our nation's prisons eventually return. The courts allocate insufficient time to serious cases, and correctional facilities offer little more than crude warehousing services for prisoners. Yet judges must deal with a wide range of petty conduct, and a large part of the population of the nation's short-term penal institutions is comprised of peaceful alcoholics.

The failure of the criminal law and the agencies of criminal justice to halt the upsurge of crime is not unrelated to the need for a redefinition of criminality. If the system were working well—if the police were apprehending most criminals, if the courts were adjudicating them efficiently, quickly, and fairly, if the correctional system were correcting—the need to divert certain categories of cases and offenders would be less compelling. But the system is too overloaded to be working well. It is within this context that we must strive to limit the responsibilities of the criminal-justice system to those antisocial acts which really pose some substantial threat to our peace and security. We may have to choose between the various goals we design for the criminal-justice system. If our compelling fear is of violent crime, then we should set appropriate priorities to deal with this problem and free the police, the courts and correctional agencies from the task of providing social, medical and welfare services.

The first reform of the criminal-justice system should be a reassessment of the definition of criminality. Serious consideration must be given to the elimination of several kinds of cases from its jurisdiction, such as public drunkenness, traffic and housing violations, possession of narcotics, gambling, obscenity, certain sex offenses. The criminal law is overextended. The heavy reliance upon it to enforce a wide variety of society's norms, besides adversely affecting the working of the system, presupposes a deterrent and rehabilitative power which in many instances simply does not exist. The criminal law has been used to regulate certain forms of conduct which are likely to be better regulated within an administrative structure; and it is often just a reflection of society's repugnance toward certain forms of relatively harmless conduct—at least relatively harmless to the public—which contravene traditional Judaeo-Christian ethics.

The criminal-justice system has been a dumping ground for society's failures in the fields of social and medical care. People are being arrested—and in larger numbers than many of us realize—simply because they need the basic necessities of life which are furnished in this nation's jails. The following is an entire newspaper story carried not long ago:

> WOMAN IS ARRESTED TO GET WARMED UP
>
> Police found an elderly woman shivering from the cold on the front porch of a home in a fashionable area of town and booked her on a vagrancy charge so she could warm up in jail. "We had to book her in order to give her a place to stay," said a police spokesman Monday.[4]

Those who may believe this news item to be unrepresentative of how criminal-justice resources are employed might consider that of the estimated total of six million arrests made in this country each year, two million are for nondisorderly public drunkenness, mostly involving persons who urgently need medical and welfare services. In 1966, after the police in New York City were instructed to stop arresting nondisorderly Skid Row derelicts, the loudest hue and cry came from those who had depended upon the food and shelter offered by the local jails.[5] Too large a proportion of arrests is intended to give medical, social and welfare care to people in need of these services and to remove from the streets people who present an obnoxious appearance to middle-class America.

Criminal caseloads, of course, should not be indiscriminately reduced merely because the courts are overloaded. The fact that they are overloaded simply underscores the need to find better alternatives for handling certain kinds of cases and offenders. The system should be revamped so that it will include only those forms of conduct and those kinds of offenders for which it is well suited. Definitive proposals in all types of cases may be difficult to make without further study, but we can speedily remove from the system some large groups of cases which clearly do not belong in it, and begin experimenting with the removal of other cases which seem unsuitable for criminal processing. Also, we ought to give a great deal more thought to finding alternatives to prosecution for certain offenders who are charged with offenses that do belong in the criminal lexicon but who, for a variety of reasons, do not require or respond adequately to the punitive features of the criminal law.

The removal of cases from the criminal system, in addition to the benefits accruing to the system itself and to the individual defendants whose cases are removed, would permit existing resources and attention to be allocated to more serious cases. Thus, in a sense, reducing the caseload compensates in some measure for the inadequacy of resources in the system.

Again, the criminal law seeks to regulate conduct which, although not serious, is clearly undesirable. Automobile traffic offenses, for example, comprise the overwhelming number of cases heard in the criminal courts. Similarly, a wide range of housing, health and sanitation offenses are also heard in the same courts that process murder, rape and mugging cases. While there is little doubt that some regulatory scheme is necessary to deal with the highly complex problems of urban life, it simply does not follow that this regulation must be entrusted to the agencies, procedures and facilities of the criminal-justice system. Many business dealings are governed by administrative agencies. The Securities and Exchange Commission, the Federal Trade Commission, the Interstate Commerce Commission and a host of state and local agencies have the authority to regulate undesirable business practices, but only the most serious of these practices are subject to the severe sanction of the criminal law. This same dual regulatory scheme can be made applicable to other forms of conduct. Ironically, because of the limited but harsh alternatives of criminal punishment, the courts have been notably ineffective in preventing undesirable practices in housing and in the use of automobiles. Given the choice between fines and jail sentences for offenses which the community does not regard as especially horrendous, judges traditionally mete out low fines which neither rehabilitate nor punish offenders, nor deter the undesirable conduct.

And, to repeat, categories of cases should not be removed from the criminal courts unless they can be processed as well or better in other agencies.

Setting wiser priorities in the use of the criminal system goes hand in hand with setting more pragmatic goals. The criminal law should be made more efficient to deal with serious crimes. It should not be used to provide medical services or temporary shelter when private and public health and welfare agencies are (or certainly should be) better equipped to perform these tasks. It should not be given the responsibilities of an administrative agency when such an agency either exists or may be formed to do a more effective job. Nor should it regulate conduct only because it offends the moral standards of a few or of even the majority of citizens.

In this "law and order" era, one of the most vocal complaints against the courts, one prompted by the frustration in not dealing effectively with offenders, is "permissiveness." "The courts are too lenient," cry public officials. "The courts are too lenient," then cry large segments of the population. And, as proof of leniency, we are shown cases of offenders, some with prior records, who are permitted to plead guilty to less serious offenses than those actually committed and who are then placed on probation or given brief prison terms.

This allegation raises some fundamental questions. First, are we willing to give to the courts the resources needed to handle properly all cases brought to them? Second, what are the considerations that should enter into the sentencing decisions? A pound of flesh from all who violate the law? If so, what are the likely results of a punitive approach to offenders? Should the sentencing judge be primarily motivated by the need to isolate offenders? If so, for what crimes and how long should they be imprisoned? What will be the effect of a punitive approach on convicted offenders who are released at a point in their lives when they can still cause considerable injury to society? Or should we use the sentencing process to try to rehabilitate offenders so that they will become productive and law-abiding members of society?

Somewhere in the lack of answers to these questions is the cause of a great deal of misunderstanding by the public. Indeed, this same misunderstanding exists among professionals within the criminal-justice system. Judges would not all agree on the answers. And different agencies of justice disagree. Frequently, the courts are criticized by the police for releasing defendants to the community both prior to trial and after conviction. With regard to detention prior to trial, should a free nation such as ours tolerate imprisonment *before* a person is convicted—when he is presumed innocent in the eyes of the law? And post-conviction imprisonment also raises troublesome questions. Should all who are convicted be imprisoned, or only those considered dangerous? Should a person who commits a serious crime be imprisoned if an inquiry into his background reveals that he would function well in society under some limited form of control and with some guidance?

Those critical of such allegedly permissive sentencing approaches as probation are deluded by the results of prison sentences. Certainly a judge can ensure that a defendant remains crime-free for three, four, perhaps seven years. But is this really the answer for a twenty-year-old defendant who will still come out of prison a young (but more hardened) man? (I suppose some would unrealistically suggest that he ought to be detained for forty years so that he will not be a danger to society.)

An assessment of sentencing alternatives would provide a better understanding of the sentencing judge's dilemma in seeking to prevent future unlawful behavior on the part of the convicted offender. In Chapter IX the description of prisons may serve to demonstrate the nature of the judge's quandary. The shortcomings of prison training programs and the unnatural and often uncivilized state of prison life preclude the use of prisons at this time for anything but punishment. This is the reason why repeated petty offenders may be sentenced more than once to a term of probation, which, despite limitations, seems to do a better job, at a lower cost, of keeping offenders out of trouble. The sentencing dilemma is intensified by overwhelmed probation staffs that can do little more than devote a few minutes each month to each offender placed in their custody.

The importance of bolstering the correctional process—to make it more meaningful in rehabilitating offenders—can hardly be overstated. We cannot wage an effective war against crime with a punitive "correctional" process. There may be times when prison sentences are necessary to provide control over dangerous people, to punish, and to deter certain of the most vicious forms of conduct. But unless we can do something more than punish offenders, we dilute the ultimate effectiveness of the apprehension process.

Our response to crime has been piecemeal. Allocations have been made without consideration of the needs of the total system. The overriding concern for police needs has had deleterious effects on the other criminal-justice components. But more arrests mean more court cases and an intolerable burden on courts, prosecutors, public defenders, and correction, probation and parole resources.

In New York City, police drives on prostitutes, resulting in dragnet arrests to clean up certain areas of Manhattan, usually culminate in court dismissals of charges due to lack of evidence. But the police continue these drives and then point to the outcome of the court proceedings as examples of coddling criminals. The courts continue to throw the cases out, often upon request of the district attorney's office, which recognizes the impossibility of proving the charges in court. But the police continue to round up suspected prostitutes. Another example is enforcement of the New York crime of loitering "for the purpose of unlawfully using or possessing a dangerous drug." Despite the intent of the law, the charges are usually impossible to prove. The police bring in suspected addicts; the courts then dismiss the charges. Under a better system the police would be guided by what happens to these cases in court.

Let me illustrate this point further by a reference to just one of the many problems confronting the courts in New York City today. The frequent inability of the Department of Correction to have prisoners in court promptly for scheduled appearances prevents the involved parties from proceeding. Judges complain that they are unable to begin on time because defendants in pretrial detention quarters are not present; the Department of Correction counters by pointing to the numerous court appearances which must be made for each detained defendant, due to the repeated adjournments in the average case. The problem transcends fixing blame and eludes simple solutions. If additional funds are needed to solve the problem, they should be made available after thorough consideration of how these funds can best be applied, with an eye to the most efficient functioning of the entire system.

Priorities, as a practical matter, must be reevaluated; instead of the several agencies competing for funds independently of one another, the funds should be allocated according to a master plan. Perhaps more buses should be provided to bring prisoners to court. Perhaps the best solution would be to modernize the scheduling procedures used by the courts. The large number of adjournments and court appearances, with resulting long-term detentions prior to trial, probably are at the core of this particular problem. If the average number of court appearances were reduced by an improved processing of cases, the Department of Correction would then have to bring prisoners to court less often than it does at present—with corresponding improvement in the caliber of the transportation services provided to the courts. Only by careful planning can it be seen that purchasing more buses to bring prisoners to court might be a shortsighted step.

Closer cooperation among the system's component parts is essential if a rational crime-control effort is to be made. These parts are so interdependent that the inadequacy of one can derange the entire system. And, conversely, the strengthening of one without regard to the effect on the others can be just as disruptive.

The problems of crime control cut across agency lines. A case proceeds through several stages of the criminal-justice system, and the attention of several agencies must be devoted to each case prior to final disposition. Proper handling of a case depends upon successful participation by each of these agencies. The absence or unpreparedness of one party to a case, whether he be the arresting officer, the public defender, the prosecutor or the probation officer, precludes proper handling. Shortages in personnel in the Police Department's narcotics laboratories have caused delays in completing reports on suspected narcotics. These delays cause adjournments and further delays in moving cases in court. Similarly, staff shortages in a public defender's or prosecutor's office (as well as unpreparedness or administrative shortcomings) are apt to delay proceedings in court despite an otherwise smoothly functioning system. The system can be no stronger than its weakest unit.

II REDEFINITION OF CRIMES: PUBLIC HEALTH AND WELFARE ALTERNATIVES

HANDLING PUBLIC DRUNKENNESS

Every year in this country there are two million arrests for public drunkenness—mostly of poor, homeless alcoholics who reside in the nation's Skid Rows. Some have been arrested hundreds of times and sentenced so often to thirty- and sixty-day jail terms that they have actually spent major portions of their lives in jail. A 1956 study of offenders being held at one time in the District of Columbia workhouse revealed that six alcoholic inmates had been arrested a total of 1,389 times and had served 125 years in jail.[1] The repeated arrest and incarceration of these derelicts has been aptly termed "life imprisonment on the installment plan."

Many of the people who are apprehended suffering from illnesses associated with heavy drinking (cardiovascular disease, tuberculosis, and cirrhosis of the liver) and from extreme poverty (malnutrition, fractured limbs, infections, influenza, and pneumonia) require medical care. When alcoholics stop drinking, they are apt to suffer from delirium tremens, with its distressing withdrawal symptoms of tremors, nausea, hallucinations and convulsions, which, if unattended, may lead to death. Homeless alcoholics die in jails, in all parts of the country, solely because they do not receive the proper attention.

Alcoholics suffering from acute intoxication require proper food and vitamin supplements, rest in a supervised setting, emergency medical supervision and medication to mitigate severe withdrawal symptoms. After regaining sobriety, the homeless alcoholic needs four or five days to "dry out," or detoxify, a process by which the body eliminates all traces of alcohol and restores itself to a reasonably normal functioning level. During this time, the alcoholic needs medical and social care which should constitute the initial phase of a possible long-range rehabilitation program. His particular problems should be diagnosed and he should be referred to an aftercare program which would seek to alter his heavy drinking patterns. Job counseling and supportive residential housing or, at the very least, overnight lodgings should be part of this early rehabilitative effort.

In 1961, a federal grant was used to establish the Cooperative Commission on Alcohol, which conducted, as part of a six-year national study, a survey of how public inebriates were being treated. Commission representatives traveled around the country inspecting the facilities and procedures used to handle this problem. They found that the jail (commonly known as the "tank") is the primary makeshift detoxification facility.

After describing jail cells for intoxicated prisoners as "very crowded, quite crude and totally inadequate from both a humane and medical standpoint," the Cooperative Commission on Alcohol concluded that "the infamous 'drunk tanks' found in almost all city jails are instances of barbaric mistreatment." [2] Medical examinations in the nation's jails are virtually nonexistent, and the only medical care generally available takes the form of transportation to public hospitals after symptoms of serious illness come to the attention of the jailers. Food is provided, but not in the particular form or quantity suited to the homeless alcoholic's needs.

A California report described the local tank as a cell holding forty to fifty men where there is "no room to sit or lie down" and "where sanitary facilities and ventilation are inadequate and a stench of vomit and urine is prevalent." It observed that although the inebriate is presumably arrested for his own protection, it is questionable whether he is not safer on the streets than in jail.[3]

In the few established detoxification centers the treatment afforded homeless alcoholics is radically different than in the nation's jails. In the Manhattan Bowery Project in New York City, begun and operated by the Vera Institute of Justice, drying out for many Skid Row alcoholics occurs in a hospital setting, supplemented by an intelligent and humane medical-social program. Teams consisting of a plainclothes policeman and a recovered alcoholic patrol the Bowery every day, offering help to alcoholics in need of treatment. Those who accept (and most who are asked do so) are transported to the project's facility for a five- or six-day stay. Upon arrival, patients are bathed, given clean clothing, clean beds, medical examinations and tests, emergency treatment, and appropriate medication to alleviate alcohol withdrawal symptoms. Deaths of alcoholics and even serious withdrawal symptoms are practically nonexistent in detoxification centers. Carefully chosen foods are provided, with high protein and vitamin and mineral supplements. During subsequent periods, emphasis is on diagnosis and referral to appropriate aftercare-treatment services. Over half of all people treated in the New York City detoxification center accept referral to some type of aftercare program at one of thirty-six agencies which participate in the program.

The notion that the penal system provides adequate detoxification care for inebriated alcoholics is inaccurate on several grounds. Jails are intended only as sobering-up facilities and cannot provide the longer stay that is necessary for detoxification. In addition, it is an inaccurate assumption that those arrested for drunkenness are those most in need of care. There is at least a dual motivation for the arrest of homeless alcoholics: first, providing shelter for impoverished, incapacitated alcoholics, and, second, a "street-cleaning" operation—removing obnoxious sights from the view of passersby and local retail businessmen. Since the most incapacitated alcoholics might not be in the public view and, conversely, the least incapacitated (but most obnoxious-looking) alcoholics might be in the public view, very often the wrong people are brought in for help. Moreover, there is some evidence that the police sometimes prefer to arrest the more easily manageable ambulatory inebriates. Arrest practices vary from city to city, and where there is strict enforcement of drunk laws in Skid Row areas many people are caught up in dragnet arrests who do not require emergency detoxification care. In other jurisdictions, people who require care are left on the streets. It is also a mistake to assume that the people in need of emergency care are receiving it in the jails. Adequate emergency services are simply not being provided in most jurisdictions either by the ill-equipped penal system or, according to the Cooperative Commission on Alcoholism, by the public hospitals and care-giving public agencies.

Fourteen years ago, Dean Allen of the University of Michigan Law School, observing that the system of criminal justice has "sometimes been employed as a device for the administration of what are essentially social services," advised:

> Whenever penal sanctions are employed to deal with problems of social service, two things are almost certain to happen and a third result may occur. First, the social services will not be effectively rendered. Second, the diversion of personnel, resources, and energy required in the effort will adversely affect the ability of a system of criminal justice to fulfill those functions that it can perform. Finally, the effort may sometimes result in the corruption and demoralization of the agencies of criminal justice.[4]

One additional generalization should be mentioned. When the criminal-justice system undertakes to provide social services, it creates for itself a virtual monopoly in the field, performing exclusively the tasks that should be performed by public and private health and social agencies. The criminal system becomes the rug under which are swept the most visible, and sometimes the most complex, social and medical problems. These problems often are so unwieldy, and government provides such inadequate resources to cope with them, that the agencies which should be responsible are quite content to leave them in the criminal-justice system.

Jailing large numbers of impoverished alcoholics also has a detrimental effect upon the criminal-justice system in two respects. It floods the underfinanced and understaffed courts and correctional facilities with cases, and it results in the deviation by the police and the courts from well-established principles of law designed to protect citizens against arbitrary government action. The enforcement of law largely against the very poor segments of society tarnishes the system's image of fairness and impartiality. A similar deteriorating influence is created by the court processing of alcoholics characterized by almost total absence of procedural rights and by emphasis on speed. Large groups of disheveled defendants are paraded each morning before our magistrates and soon thereafter herded into Correction Department vans or back to Skid Row to continue their destructive drinking habits.

The practice of arresting and convicting homeless alcoholics for public drunkenness has been challenged over the past few years. In 1966, two federal appeals courts ruled that the conviction of homeless alcoholics would no longer be tolerated.[5] One of the decisions, in *Driver v. Hinnant,* involving a defendant convicted of public intoxication more than two hundred times, was based on the rationale that chronic alcoholism is an addictive disease, that the victim's appearance in public in a drunken condition is unwilled and ungovernable, and that therefore to brand him a criminal is "cruel and unusual punishment" in violation of the United States Constitution.[6] The federal court in that case was influenced by an earlier United States Supreme Court decision, in *Robinson v. California,* which held in effect that the status of being addicted to narcotics could not constitutionally be legislated as criminal behavior.[7] Other courts, upholding the public-drunkenness convictions of alcoholics, have observed that the earlier *Robinson* decision referred only to a law punishing addiction as such and did not proscribe the act of possessing drugs as criminal behavior.

In 1968, the United States Supreme Court, in *Powell v. Texas,*[8] was asked to adopt the rationale of the earlier federal court decisions which had held the public-drunkenness laws unconstitutional. The case involved the conviction of Leroy Powell, an alcoholic who had been arrested for the crime of public drunkenness on seventy to one hundred prior occasions. The court affirmed Powell's conviction in a five–four decision, refusing to extend the rationale of cruel and unusual punishment to the public drunkenness of alcoholics. The four dissenting justices observed that since it would be unconstitutional to convict an alcoholic for his alcoholism, it was just as unlawful to convict him for the symptoms (drunkenness) of his alcoholism.

Four of the justices voting to affirm Mr. Powell's conviction pointed to the lack of available and effective public-health alternatives to the arrest and jailing of homeless alcoholics. They stated: "It would be tragic to return large numbers of helpless, sometimes dangerous and frequently unsanitary inebriates to the streets of our cities without even the opportunity to sober up adequately which a brief jail term provides." [9]

Apart from the accuracy of the court's observation, it is doubtful whether the criminal law should be used to provide sobering-up services for alcoholics even if such services are adequate. The idea that it should even attempt to provide these services is contrary to the basic notions, function and design of the criminal law. After all, we would not tolerate a system that required arrest and prosecution only because jails offered the only accommodations for people suffering in public from epilepsy, heart seizures or broken arms. But when we consider that the services being provided within the criminal-justice system are less than adequate, and that the system is burdened with the difficult problem of rising crime, it is even clearer that neither the individual alcoholic nor criminal justice is aided by the continued retention of jurisdiction over what is obviously a health problem.

Whether the United States Supreme Court will in the near future put an end to the practice of arresting alcoholics for public intoxication is subject to speculation. Its five–four decision in the 1968 case of *Powell v. Texas* gives some indication that it might. Associate Justice Byron R. White, one of the five justices voting to uphold Powell's conviction, distinguished in his concurring opinion between a homeless alcoholic who had no choice but to be drunk *in public* and an alcoholic with a home who was not compelled to be in public when drunk. Mr. Powell, he said, was not homeless and therefore did not have to be in public when arrested. It is noteworthy that most people arrested for this offense *are* homeless.

In *Powell v. Texas,* Associate Justice Thurgood Marshall observed that effective alternative public-health facilities have not been established. Time is needed to raise substantial amounts of funding for detoxification centers, and the court may have been providing time to develop rational alternatives. It may not wait too long before it thrusts a change on the nation. Of particular importance in this regard is the increasing number of detoxification centers being established as alternatives to the jail. As reports become available of the services provided and the success achieved in the handling of alcoholics, it is not unlikely that the court will look to these detoxification centers as appropriate alternatives to the more traditional procedures currently employed.

More diverse legal challenges are needed to compel proper handling of public-health problems. It is surprising that the entire emphasis thus far has been on the "disease" concept of alcoholism. The serious constitutional problems appear to provide ample grounds upon which to challenge the implementation of these laws. The National Crime Commission documented the very clear emphasis on arresting and convicting only poor inebriates. Police training manuals candidly distinguish between classes of citizens in the implementation of drunkenness laws. The Commission noted that in Chicago nearly all arrests for public drunkenness are unsupportable, since there did not happen to be a public-drunkenness law applicable. In several states, high-court decisions have suggested that public drunkenness is *not* a sufficient basis for conviction for that offense in the absence of disorderly conduct. In other areas, arrests have continued despite high-court rulings to the contrary, largely because the people arrested have not been financially able to afford counsel.

In New York City, there has been some success in terminating police arrests of homeless alcoholics by encouraging the participation of lawyers in these cases. In 1965, at a time when no public-intoxication law was applicable, an experimental project was instituted to determine whether the arrests of derelicts for disorderly conduct could be supported by requisite evidence of breach of the peace. Legal Aid Society attorneys were assigned to cases of Skid Row residents, and it was found that acquittals resulted in approximately ninety-five percent of all cases. Prior to this experiment, in ninety-five percent of the cases there had been convictions, almost all by pleas of guilty. As a result of the experiment, the courts refused to process complaints against Skid Row residents unless the charge of disorderly conduct could be supported by disorderly behavior as defined by generations of case law. The Police Department then instructed its personnel to refrain from arresting nondisorderly inebriates. Since that time, and with the subsequent establishment of a detoxification center, the number of arrests of derelicts has been reduced in New York City from fifty thousand to six thousand each year. This number has remained relatively constant despite the subsequent passage of a public-intoxication law.

The value of bringing legal challenges to existing law-enforcement procedures is that they are the readiest and most potent instruments for spurring necessary reforms and rescuing the criminal-justice system from being used as a substitute for a public-health program. It is not surprising that this country came closest to substituting public-health alternatives following the two highly publicized lower federal-court decisions in 1966 reversing public-drunkenness convictions. Communities were faced with pending crises and were compelled to consider the establishment of detoxification treatment facilities to replace the crude "tanks" in the local jails.

Only a small fraction of homeless alcoholics are being treated in detoxification centers, even in those cities where they have been established. The reason is money—or, more precisely, the unavailability of it for this low-priority service. Information is lacking concerning the dollar amount of criminal-justice resources which could be preserved for other matters if this public-health problem were handled within a civil framework. One of the few estimates available comes from the District of Columbia, where a Presidential crime commission concluded that approximately three million dollars were being spent in that jurisdiction to arrest, adjudicate and incarcerate more than forty thousand public-drunkenness defendants each year.[10] Unquestionably, there cannot be a net savings in money for any jurisdiction which sets up an alternative noncriminal approach. It must cost money. In return, however, there will be a much wiser use of time by police, the courts, and other criminal-justice agencies, and more humane handling of people in need of social and medical care.

HANDLING NARCOTICS ADDICTION

The second major public-health problem handled largely by agencies of criminal justice is heroin addiction, a major cause of crime in the large urban centers of the country. It is estimated that fifty thousand to one hundred thousand heroin addicts reside in New York City and that half of all defendants prosecuted for crime in New York City are heroin addicts. The New York State Narcotics Addiction Control Commission has estimated that addicts spend on the average of thirty dollars per day for heroin, and must steal property worth three to five times this amount to convert it into cash. Every addict in New York City who needs money to pay for the drug is believed to be stealing about $35,000 each year. The total amount stolen by addicts in this one city in staggering; one source puts the amount at ten million dollars each day.[11]

In assessing the drug problem and its impact on the criminal-justice system, it is important to dispel certain myths about heroin addiction. There is nothing about the use of heroin itself which produces serious criminal behavior. Contrary to the notion prevalent two or three decades ago that the addict is aggressively motivated to commit crimes of violence as a result of the physiological reaction to the drug, its actual effect is a general reduction of the level of bodily activity. As an opiate, heroin is a depressant, the use of which produces a tendency to inactivity and lethargy.

The use of heroin leads to violation of law in two major respects: (1) by definition, the possession or sale of the drug is punishable criminally; and (2) the uncontrollable and continuous need for the drug, coupled with the high cost of acquiring it, compels addicts to commit crimes to obtain funds for its purchase. The latter factor, particularly, is responsible for much of the crime in our larger cities—an estimated fifty percent of the serious crimes in New York City, for example.

The possession of alcohol is not illegal, hence no definitional crime problem exists there as with heroin. Alcohol is readily available at low cost to the consumer as compared to the cost of illicit drugs; hence, unlike the heroin addict, the alcoholic is not compelled to commit crimes to pay for the drug to which he is addicted. Alcohol consumption, however, has a far greater crime-producing effect than heroin use, because it generates a higher level of nervous and other bodily activity. Studies have shown that a large percentage of violent crime is alcohol-related.[12] Homicide and forcible rape, for example, are often committed by people under the influence of alcohol. Available evidence indicates that even when driven by their habit to obtain funds, heroin addicts generally commit property crimes, although sometimes they will resort to violence. It is also noteworthy that because heroin depresses sexual activity, heroin addicts commit relatively few sexual crimes.

The arrest of public-drunkenness offenders is rationalized by the benefits offered them by the arrest-court-corrections process. No such justification is offered in defense of the arrest of narcotics addicts. There is no pretense that the criminal law, by itself, fills the unmet needs of narcotics addicts, and it is clear, far clearer than in the case of alcoholics, that the criminal system offers little to the individual addict. After being arrested and detained, the addict faces withdrawal without medical assistance; and in most cases, the withdrawal agonies are more severe than they are for alcoholics. The addict is simply stored in a penal setting—in a place where he poses no threat to society—and ultimately released. As in the case of the homeless alcoholic, the heroin addict is apt to be arrested repeatedly and to spend substantial periods of time in detention on short-term sentences. Unlike public drunkenness, which seldom rises to the level of a misdemeanor, drug possession and drug vending are more serious crimes—misdemeanors and felonies carrying a potential of severe sentences. And for the most part, nothing is being done within the correctional institutions themselves to treat the addict or to discover the cause of his addiction.

The intense and growing demand for heroin, combined with its unavailability through legal sources, results in high profits for organized crime syndicates which import, distribute and sell the drug in disregard of the inherent risks involved. Reaching those who engage in the importation, distribution and sale of heroin, and seizing large quantities of the drug are two objectives of law enforcement almost impossible to achieve. There are no witnesses to these clandestine operations, no victims—as we generally use the term—only willing buyers who desperately need the product and their sources of supply.

In order to achieve their goals, police personnel initiate investigations and rely on a variety of unconventional and often undesirable enforcement procedures. Officers mask their identities and pose as addicts and attempt to develop leads to possible informants who would be able to provide necessary information. An unholy alliance of police officers and underworld figures has developed in an attempt by police to gain information about these illegal operations. Informants are paid by the police in some cases, and in others they are induced to give information in return for favorable adjustments of cases pending against them.

Because many addicts are compelled to sell narcotics in order to raise necessary funds, they are the most vulnerable for arrest and prosecution. Although arrests of addicts for selling heroin are quite common, little success has been achieved in apprehending the large distributors. Much of the law-enforcement focus in the drug area has been on apprehending the slum resident user-seller of heroin. The quality of drug arrests is revealed by an analysis made of 72,000 such arrests in 1970. Two thirds resulted in misdemeanor charges. Of those, two thirds of the possession charges and nine tenths of the drug-loitering charges resulted in dismissals.[13]

The demands placed upon law-enforcement personnel to produce results lead to widespread violations of law by police. Illegal searches of citizens, their homes and their automobiles are one example. Another is perjured police testimony designed to permit the use of evidence seized in violation of constitutional safeguards.

Prior to a 1961 United States Supreme Court ruling, evidence illegally seized from defendants could be used in state and local courts to establish guilt. Illegally seized evidence was admissible despite police testimony that it had been secured in violation of the Fourth Amendment to the United States Constitution. But after the court ruled this type of evidence inadmissible,[14] a large number of "dropsy" cases suddenly appeared on the scene. In such cases the typical allegation is that as the policeman approached the defendant he dropped the contraband (such as a gun, narcotics or gambling slips) to the ground. The allegation is that the police, observing the abandoned material, picked it up, inspected it and then placed the defendant under arrest. There are variations, of course. Sometimes there are two or more defendants. Sometimes the defendant stands still (obediently awaiting the police perusal of the illegally possessed material); sometimes he is alleged to have walked away. In order to establish the possession of the contraband the police officer testifies that he never lost sight of it from the time it left the defendant's hand to the time it was retrieved.

Most knowledgeable observers recognize the high incidence of perjury in these dropsy cases. Recently the distinguished District Attorney of New York County, Frank S. Hogan, in a brief submitted to the courts, acknowledged that "in a substantial but indeterminable" number of dropsy cases the testimony "is tailored to meet the requirements of search and seizure rulings." [15] The problem for the trial courts is that not all such allegations are false and that, as suggested in Mr. Hogan's brief, "it is very difficult in many cases to distinguish between fact and fiction."

Also, because of the potential for huge monetary gain, police corruption is believed to be prevalent. Narcotics sellers pay for immunity from arrest, and large amounts of drugs obtained by police are sometimes rechanneled into illicit markets. This is only part of the price which we pay for placing such heavy reliance upon combatting this problem through law enforcement.

Heroin addiction as such cannot constitutionally be criminally punishable. In 1962 the United States Supreme Court in *Robinson v. California* ruled that it is cruel and unusual punishment to punish the "illness" of addiction.[16] This 1962 Supreme Court case is consistent with informed medical opinion that drug addiction is a medical problem and that the addict who stops using heroin faces severe and distressing withdrawal symptoms.

In the light of the data on heroin addiction, it is obvious that the criminal law cannot control the narcotics traffic or offer the hope of deterring addicts from committing crimes to obtain funds. The deep physiological and psychological drives to use heroin, if only to be free from the ordeal of withdrawal, transcend the fear of apprehension, conviction and institutionalization. The purportedly deterrent feature of the criminal law is simply irrelevant to the addict who needs money to purchase heroin. The available medical data provide sufficient basis to argue that narcotics addicts find it impossible to restrain themselves from committing crimes when necessary to raise funds for their habit. Narcotics addicts, by definition, must at least commit the crime of possession of narcotics. One Supreme Court justice has suggested that the logic of the *Robinson* decision, based as it is on the premise that addicts must use drugs, is applicable to the possession of drugs by addicts. The Supreme Court itself has never been required to determine that issue.

In any event, all of the available evidence establishes that the criminal law cannot be relied on to control addiction-related crime. And it makes little sense to arrest and detain addicts for a few months or even years and then release them, unprotected and unsupervised, to the same environment within which they used narcotics in the first place. Invariably they will use the drug again.

The ultimate retail prices of illicit drug sales are enormous—almost one billion dollars a year in New York City alone. These prices create a series of staggering profits at each stage, from the sale of the crops in Turkey to the initial processing into heroin, to the final sale in slum areas. Were an entire drug syndicate put behind bars—a most unlikely event—another one would spring up in a matter of weeks.

Perhaps the cruelest irony of relying on law enforcement to combat addiction-related crime is that the more efficient law enforcement becomes, the higher the price for the diminished supply, and the greater the need for money to pay the higher prices. Thus, efficiency in law enforcement has the anomalous effect of causing more crime.

CIVIL COMMITMENT OF ALCOHOL AND DRUG ADDICTS

One of the most obvious alternatives to the criminal system is involuntary hospitalization. The theory behind this alternative is fairly simple: If a criminal act is not voluntary, if it is the result of a sick mind or in any way the symptom of a sickness, it should not be the subject of criminal punishment. One view is that sick people who commit crimes need treatment and, therefore, should be hospitalized. Added to this is the more pragmatic and often more honest reason behind involuntary hospitalization: As long as a sick person remains a threat to society he will be detained—if not in a jail, then in something that is apt to resemble a jail.

Civil-commitment laws describe the circumstances under which persons may be involuntarily hospitalized. Some insist upon a showing that the person is dangerous; others refer only to the need for treatment in a residential setting. The decision to hospitalize for any substantial period of time must be made by a court following a hearing at which evidence is presented. Over the past few years the rights of patients have been enlarged. Some states are providing for the right to counsel and the right to periodic review of the decision to continue hospitalization.

Committing people under the civil law to a hospital instead of sentencing them under the criminal law to jail is fraught with many dangers. Experience with hospitalization of the mentally ill has shown that there are fewer safeguards against long-term confinement and other abuses than there are under the criminal law. It has also shown that in these hospitals there is a greater emphasis on confinement than on treatment. Periodic reports of twenty- to forty-year hospitalization of people charged with petty crimes—often people who had been committed to institutions because they were mentally incompetent to stand trial—present the most graphic examples of the danger of civil commitment.

While the use of civil-commitment laws may be necessary in

some instances in dealing with mentally deranged people who commit acts of violence, its extension to the public-health problems under discussion here should not be tolerated without the most careful consideration of the likely consequences. The experience in Washington, D.C., following the 1966 federal court decision in that district is instructive. The local courts committed homeless alcoholics to the District of Columbia Department of Public Health under a civil-commitment statute. In order to house these people, part of the local workhouse was set aside as a "health facility" for alcoholics. Thus, homeless alcoholics were sent as "patients" to the same institution which had housed them as prisoners for many years. In testimony taken during a hearing on a motion to vacate previous judicial orders civilly committing twenty-five homeless alcoholics to the Department of Public Health, one of the patients testified that there were two essential differences in his being detained as a civil patient as compared to his previous incarcerations as a prisoner on criminal charges. The first was that his uniform was changed from gray to white, the second concerned the degree of freedom permitted within the institution: as prisoners, the alcoholics had access to all of the recreational facilities in the institution; as patients, they had to be kept separated from the prisoners, and, since the prisoners had access to the recreational facilities, the patients were kept locked in their dormitories.

The director of the District of Columbia Department of Correction, upon being asked whether alcoholics were locked in their dormitories without recreational privileges, gave the following testimony:

It is customary to lock dormitories when there appears to be a need to do so. The locking consists of a little hatch that was put on the door to—in an attempt mostly, to keep these men separated from the other inmates. As you know, the inmates do have free access around the institution. While they are reasonably controlled, they do wander around somewhat. We are under an order from the Board of Commissioners to accommodate these men separate and apart . . . from the other convicted inmates . . . This we attempted to do.[17]

Needless to say, the local courts in Washington, D.C., acted quickly to terminate the practice of using a penal institution as a civil health facility. Other examples, while less graphic than the situation in Washington, D.C., unfortunately exist of confinement in hospitals bearing a remarkable resemblance to confinement in jails.

State-operated mental hospitals often take on the same physical characteristics as jails: overcrowding in dingy, drab quarters, bars on the windows, a minimum of recreational and rehabilitation programs, long-term detention. Similarly, it is no wonder to sophisticated observers why addicts in New York City's courts prefer criminal rather than civil processing. For one thing, detention time is usually longer under the state's civil-commitment program. Many of the addicts who are committed complain of jail-like conditions. In a letter to the New York City Legal Aid Society one addict who had been civilly committed said, "I'm being treated like an animal in a locked cage." [18]

Under the California and New York commitment laws, the maximum confinement is dependent upon the underlying crime classification: three years for misdemeanants, five years for felons. Obviously, in a rehabilitation program there is no logical correlation between length of commitment and the crime for which the addict was convicted. Tying the length of commitment to the crime lends credence to the views of those who charge that the commitment programs in California and New York are aimed at removing (and keeping) addicts from the streets.

Apart from the element of long-term detention, the New York commitment program has been compared to a prison. Complaints of inactivity, severe overcrowding, homosexuality, rigid rules, staff shortages and occasional brutality are common. The difference between goals and reality was highlighted by a letter from an addict which stated: ". . . the man told me that I would go to a hospital with psychologists, psychiatrists and doctors. They told me it would be just like home . . . Sometimes I feel like I'm in a terrible nightmare." [19]

Narcotics-addiction commitment programs have a history of failure. Both the California and the federal programs have had little success in curing addicts despite long periods of detention without the use of drugs. Only five percent of all people in the California program remained drug free for three years after fifty-four months of institutionalization. The one lesson learned from available statistics is that addicts go right back to their old drug habits after being released from public health facilities.

The United States Supreme Court in the 1968 *Powell v. Texas* decision voiced apprehension concerning the use of civil commitment as a means of continuing to lock up addicts while denying them the full extent of the traditional protection of the criminal system. The Court stated:

> One virtue of the criminal process is, at least, that the duration of penal incarceration typically has some outside statutory limit; this is universally true in the case of petty offenses, such as public drunkenness, where jail terms are quite short on the whole. "Therapeutic civil commitment" lacks this feature; one is typically committed until one is "cured." [This] . . . might subject indigent alcoholics to the risk that they may be locked up for an indefinite period of time under the same conditions as before, with no more hope than before of receiving effective treatment and no prospect of periodic "freedom." [20]

The likely adoption of civil-commitment laws in the event that criminal laws are repealed or ruled invalid goes to the heart of the problem. Only by establishing a true alternative to the criminal system, with a variety of public-health services, can we really achieve the desired change. Otherwise, there will be a change only in labels, with detention continuing to be the most prominent feature of the program. An underlying rationale of drunkenness arrests is that through the criminal system we remove unattractive people from the streets and give them necessary care. If drunkenness laws were repealed today, the same reasons for arresting homeless alcoholics would continue to exist. It is reasonable to assume that a convenient alternative would be sought and civil commitment would be that alternative. Similarly, there is a prevailing policy to remove narcotics addicts from the streets. We would accomplish little by striking down criminal laws which incarcerate addicts while permitting the same policies to be continued through a civil-commitment program.

FINDING RATIONAL ALTERNATIVES TO THE JAILING OF ALCOHOL AND DRUG ADDICTS

The prospect of finding some scientific cure to relieve the suffering of addicts and permit them to lead normal, productive lives is not an unrealistic one. Research in this area should be expanded, and the future might bring us the relief so desperately needed. In the meantime, we must pursue short-term goals for more appropriate handling of alcohol and drug addicts.

The alcohol addict is not much of a threat to our safety. He is a public nuisance and he clogs the courts and jails by his repeated arrests. The establishment of detoxification centers, supported by a network of aftercare facilities, would provide an effective replacement for the criminal system. While it appears inexpensive to send an individual alcoholic through the criminal system for a short drying-out period, the aggregate cost is substantial when we consider the large number of times this process is repeated during the average homeless alcoholic's lifetime. It might be less expensive to treat properly all homeless alcoholics; some would be cured who otherwise would spend much of their lives being shuttled in and out of the revolving door of the local jails. The saving in time and energy of criminal-justice personnel, which could be intelligently allocated to combatting serious criminality, is also worth considering in terms of costs.

More complex problems are presented in finding substitute programs for the arrest and conviction of narcotics addicts. But experimental, action-oriented programs supplemented by a variety of educational efforts can and must be developed. These programs will be expensive because they will require, in some cases, the immediate expenditure of substantial amounts of funds. Over the long run, however, these initial costs may be lower than under the wasteful methods presently employed. One of the great virtues of the New York State program is that it encompasses a wide range of attempts to develop treatment programs. Although the state program is often identified with civil commitment, in actuality several different kinds of noncommitment programs are being funded. The many different types of addicts with varying degrees of backgrounds and motivation to get off drugs underscore the need for such diversity in experimentation.

One method of experimentation which we turn to out of necessity for short-term results is dispensing free narcotics. We cannot wait until the medical profession finds a successful treatment for addiction, although every possible effort should be made to achieve this goal. Bold steps must be taken on an experimental basis to remove the addict's need to raise large sums of money for drugs. If he must, the addict will always find ways to raise funds—ways which tend to corrupt our criminal-justice system and threaten our property and safety. Maintenance programs should be tried during this crisis period to determine whether addicts can be relieved from the pressures driving them to commit crimes.

Methadone is an addicting narcotic which serves as an alternative to heroin. Given in proper doses over a period of time, for most addicts it appears to have the effect of blocking the desire for heroin and even of blocking the euphoric effect of heroin if the addict attempts to use both drugs. Most important, it may be easily administered orally at a cost of a few cents per day. Unlike heroin addicts, those who use methadone are able to function as normal individuals and can plan constructively for their future lives. After tolerance to methadone has been established, the dose can be held constant, without escalation, for years. Limited studies conducted to date reveal that large doses of methadone have been remarkably successful in keeping addicts off heroin. With the help of methadone, they are no longer compelled to become petty thieves and muggers to pay for the expensive habit of heroin addiction.

Despite criticism that methadone merely replaces one addiction for another, the use of methadone has enabled many addicts to live normal lives without the need to commit crimes. Studies have revealed marked reductions in criminal convictions after the admission of addicts to methadone programs. The value of methadone and the importance of expanding methadone maintenance programs emerge from the success rates of these attempts to treat addicts. As compared to an estimated eighty to ninety percent rate of failure in most other programs, large dosages of methadone in one experiment have kept eighty-two percent of addicts off heroin over a six-year period, and the eighteen percent representing the failures dropped out of the program for a variety of reasons not necessarily related to resumption of the heroin habit.[21] All who continued to take methadone, however, appear to have escaped the craving for heroin and to have again begun leading useful lives—working, attending school, performing household duties and the like.

The remarkable difference in success rates should compel us to explore on an expanded scale so promising a treatment regimen. In Los Angeles, 1,700 heroin addicts are on methadone maintenance at three clinics. When the program started, only forty percent of those accepted held steady jobs or attended school. Six months later, this rate more than doubled. Unfortunately, because of limited facilities and resources, there has been an eighteen- to twenty-four-month waiting period in some areas for addicts who desire this substitute drug. A great deal of crime is committed by heroin addicts in two years.

At the present time a methadone maintenance program (Dole-Nyswander) is operating out of several New York City hospitals.

This program consists of two phases. The first is a six-week inpatient period during which the addict is withdrawn from heroin and given a stabilized dosage of methadone. The second phase is an indefinite outpatient period in which the patient receives regular methadone dosages and supportive services. During early stages of the second phase patients return to the outpatient clinic each day to take supervised doses of methadone. Daily urine samples are taken for analysis of any traces of illicit drugs. After a while patients receive several days' dosage at a time. In addition, psychological, social and vocational counseling is provided.

The present programs are not designed to withdraw addicts from methadone. Indications are that the hunger for heroin would soon return. The encouraging results achieved to date from the use of methadone can continue only with long-term, perhaps permanent, consumption of the drug.

Recent studies have revealed that methadone addicts have not remained altogether drug-free. Eleven percent in one study were found to have used amphetamines or barbiturates, and five percent had chronic alcohol problems. There is also some evidence of heroin abuse among patients who continue taking methadone. One study revealed that thirty-five percent of methadone patients used heroin at one time or another during their methadone maintenance. But none of these has become re-addicted to heroin. The report of the study noted that "while in a maintenance program, the patient need never be afraid of going into withdrawal or becoming 'sick.' "[22] The report also found that "while 85.7% [of methadone patients] had been arrested prior to treatment, only 1.7% had been arrested at any time during their methadone treatment period (a median of 18 months)."

The most controversial maintenance program under consideration involves the distribution of heroin to hard-core addicts who lack the motivation to participate in any other treatment program. As this chapter was being written, a story was published in the New York City press concerning a purported experimental plan to provide heroin as part of a broader treatment program. The reaction was violent. Concerned people, some from the black slum areas hardest hit by heroin addiction, lashed out at the program as a "cruel hoax," "immoral" and an instrument of "colonialization." The charge was made that this would be the first step toward a legalized heroin maintenance program similar to the British system, which was roundly condemned.

In Great Britain, heroin is given to addicts by physicians, and recent reports indicate that there is a growing dissatisfaction because of the increase of addiction and the serious moral questions involved in dispensing heroin while not attempting to terminate the addiction. It seems clear from the British experience that chances are slim of medically removing addicts from drugs by lowering the dosage. Addicts in Britain are on a maintenance program and few have been cured. But there is relatively little drug-related crime in that country.

Dispensing free heroin is not a simple solution to the problems of addiction and high crime rates. Apart from the widespread hostility to this idea, several troublesome questions may properly be raised. It is said, for example, that tolerance levels are difficult to reach. Heroin addicts have ever-pressing needs for larger quantities of the drug, and there comes a point at which overdoses can kill. But this does not appear to be an insurmountable problem. Individual addicts have been obtaining heroin through illegal means for many years without reaching dosage levels beyond which death would occur. Apparently, dosages can be reduced, raised and then reduced again, while blunting if not fully satisfying the craving of the addiction. We need to know more about these tolerance levels and whether addicts can be kept on a maintenance dosage of heroin which would permit them to function usefully in the community. We should not dismiss out of hand the need for establishment of carefully supervised clinics on an experimental basis to dispense heroin to poorly motivated addicts, and for the expansion of methadone maintenance programs for highly motivated addicts.

III REDEFINITION OF CRIMES: ADMINISTRATIVE ALTERNATIVES

The highly complex problems of city life obviously require a wide range of legislatively imposed regulations. Health, sanitation, housing and traffic codes are only a few of the many regulatory schemes essential to protect residents of medium-sized and large urban areas. At first blush it may appear that the important purposes of these laws require that their infringement be punishable by imprisonment. Accordingly, we have given jurisdiction over those who violate these codes to the criminal courts.

The irony of assigning this responsibility to the criminal courts is that in many instances these infractions have been handled with neither the severity nor the efficiency which formed the basis for the assignment in the first place. Furthermore, these codes generate so many cases that a substantial portion of the courts' resources is siphoned off from more serious cases. From our experience in New York City, traffic, housing and similar minor code violations have comprised the vast bulk of the Criminal Court's caseload; and a closer look at each might provide some notion of how better alternatives for handling them can be devised.

TRAFFIC OFFENSES

There are more than 100 million drivers in the United States, driving more than 75 million vehicles about 800 billion miles annually. One of every three drivers is cited for a traffic infraction each year. And as the need to regulate grows, the rate of violations is apt to increase in the future. Already the country's traffic courts, especially in our large cities, are staggering under the burden of this tremendous caseload. In recent years, for example, the New York City Criminal Court, in addition to its heavy calendar of more serious charges, had been handling over 800,000 moving violations and over 3.2 million nonmoving violations annually. These four million cases have accounted for approximately ninety percent of all cases processed in that court. And partially because a major portion of the court's time cannot be made available for these cases, the courts that are devoted to traffic matters have been criticized more than any other for lacking "deference, dignity and decorum."

"Assembly-line justice"—a phrase used to describe the operation of the nation's lower criminal courts—is most applicable to the harassed traffic courts where throngs of accused violators are cajoled into pleading guilty each day so that the courtrooms can be emptied for the next day's onslaught. And if there is one basic principle of judicial administration which cannot be questioned it is that as caseloads and resulting pressures increase, the quality of justice and the appearance of justice decrease. In some jurisdictions, defendants are placed in unending lines and then required to shuffle past the presiding judge, who listens to their pleas of guilty and directs them to a nearby window to pay their fines. In many instances, rewards in the form of lighter fines are given for speedy guilty pleas. Lengthy explanations are unwelcome, and it is not unusual for an explanation to be followed by a higher fine than is given in the case of a guilty plea with no explanation.

In one evening in the New York City Criminal Court a few years ago, in a part of court devoted to the handling of traffic offenses, 1,882 cases were processed through a five-hour shift with two judges sitting. There were 1,330 personal appearances, and in the vast majority of these there were final dispositions. Thus, an average of approximately twenty-five seconds was afforded to each defendant who appeared in court. It has been aptly observed that the image of justice as a blindfolded lady is being transformed by the traffic courts into a "hard-faced harridan punching a cash register." [1]

It is unfortunate that the worst-run courts are those in which most of the public appears at one time or another. The nation's so-called lower criminal courts, especially those devoted to traffic cases, are in public view more than any other and depict to millions of law-abiding citizens a deteriorated court system. Comparatively few Americans visit the nation's courts of general or appellate jurisdiction, where the usually impressive physical facilities and relatively small caseloads reveal to the public eye what might properly be regarded as dignified judicial proceedings. In this era of preoccupation with respect for law and order, we ought to be concerned with improving all of the component parts of the criminal-justice system so that it may command respect. It is fruitless and hypocritical to preach the need to respect "law and order" to a person who has been shuttled through, or who has even witnessed, a chaotic court session which lasted all of one or two minutes. Dignified and orderly procedures in the nation's lower criminal courts might do much to promote respect for law among the millions who view these courts as representative of the American judicial system.

In 1969, in New York City, nearly half of all persons cited for traffic infractions flouted the law, refusing with impunity to answer citations to appear in court. Others played the system's obvious weakness to avoid answering the charges: they simply pleaded not guilty and were given trial dates thirteen months in advance (so enormous was the delay in reaching trial), at the expiration of which time they found another excuse for failing to appear, thereby receiving another thirteen-month adjournment. City officials became distressed at the large revenue being lost by people's ignoring parking tickets and notices to appear in court. Bench warrants issued by the courts were never executed by the police, because of their heavy volume and the insufficient personnel assigned to this task; and word apparently spread that answering a parking summons was a voluntary and, perhaps, public-spirited gesture which would not be enforced.

Against this background, the city and state of New York sought legislation removing jurisdiction over traffic offenses from the courts. On July 1, 1970, two new laws combined to remove all but traffic misdemeanors and felonies—such as reckless driving and automobile homicides—from the courts, giving jurisdiction of standing, stopping and parking offenses to a city administrative tribunal, and transferring moving violations such as speeding to a counterpart state agency. It has been estimated that when existing backlogs have diminished, the new administrative structure will free eighteen Criminal Court judges to hear more serious criminal matters and, because of streamlined procedures, will reduce the time policemen spend waiting in courts by one hundred thousand man-hours annually.

The new system is expected to reduce noncompliance with court summonses and to improve collection methods, which will hopefully result in the payment of millions of dollars in fines presently not being collected. Moreover, many wasted hours spent in court by drivers will be replaced by a system which permits those charged with infractions to either plead guilty by mail or choose convenient times for administrative hearings at convenient locations. A prearranged schedule of fines encourages prompt compliance by guilty respondents, as does the power to suspend licenses for failure to appear or respond to the charges. Additional fines are levied for failure to plead on time and may be imposed for failure to appear at scheduled hearings. The rights of respondents are amply safeguarded, and the procedures appear to comply with due process in every regard. Of course, a person who feels he has been treated unfairly may appeal to the courts for a review of the administrative determination.

This is the first known attempt in the nation to remove these offenses from the courts, and it will be closely examined to determine whether it measures up to the predictions made by the city. If it is more successful than the courts have been, apart from whether it achieves all of its prescribed goals, the impact on the nation's criminal-justice systems will be substantial. Even a limited success will stimulate interest in finding similar alternatives for other regulatory measures which do not warrant the stigma of the criminal sanction. Initial indications are that traffic cases are now being processed more quickly, more efficiently and with less inconvenience to the public.

HOUSING VIOLATIONS

The emphasis on speed in the processing of cases is not an exclusive feature of the nation's traffic courts; it is equally applicable to large-city housing courts where landlords are charged with evading housing codes. The major difference between the two is that housing-code prosecutions are characterized by long delays, numerous adjournments, and guilty pleas by corporate defendants. The full force of the law, including heavy fines, imprisonment, and probationary sentences are available but rarely invoked because of judicial reluctance to treat "negligent" property owners as criminals. The assistant corporation counsel in charge of housing-violation prosecutions in New York City remembers only three prison sentences meted out during the past five years out of the 91,833 such cases prosecuted in the Criminal Court of the City of New York; and those three cases involved conduct far more serious than represented by the average building violations handled in the courts.

In recent years, as crime has become a more serious problem, and as reduction of charges and plea negotiations have become more prevalent, lower-court dockets have contained many more serious crimes. It is not uncommon in some large city courts for misdemeanor cases to include a sprinkling of serious assaults, possession of weapons and stabbings, as well as larcenies currently depicted in legal texts as robberies—all reduced for a variety of reasons from the technically more appropriate felony charges. Judges understandably have great difficulty in viewing housing-code violations, as well as traffic, sanitation, and health infractions, in the same light as what they regard as the more serious charges presented in their courts. They have less patience with the processing of these violations and are less willing than in other cases to listen to elaborate explanations and defenses. Trials are frowned on because of what judges regard as the relative unimportance of these cases, as evidenced by ultimate fines of five to fifteen dollars. The beleaguered criminal courts have no means, and often lack jurisdiction, to follow through and ensure that violations are corrected.

The goal of housing-code enforcement, and I would be the last one to minimize it, is to restore and maintain healthful and decent housing conditions in existing dwellings. The criminal sanction contemplates the punishment and, in some cases, rehabilitation of offenders. This apparent inconsistency explains why the criminal sanction does not deal effectively with housing-code violations. In practice, there is little deterrent value in applying the criminal sanction to housing violations. The corporate structure can tolerate an endless number of convictions without feeling embarrassed or in any way stigmatized, and light fines are only a fraction of the cost of repairs; in fact, they appear to be regarded by some landlords as part of the overhead and operating costs. Besides, punishing the property owner does not carry out the housing-code goal of repairing the property, and a criminal court's power simply does not extend to ordering that repairs be made. Nor would it command the resources to ensure that such directives would be obeyed. Some owners fail to make repairs during the entire time the case is pending in court, until shortly before sentencing.

The city of New York attempted to achieve at the last session of the state legislature a transfer of housing-code violations from the criminal courts to an administrative tribunal. While the bill failed to become law, considerable pressure is mounting to find a suitable alternative. Criminal prosecution should be retained only for a limited group of cases in which willful and egregious refusal to comply with the law is evident.

The imposition of heavy civil penalties for housing-code violations, with full regard to due process and the right to review of administrative decisions by the courts, should be considered. Penalties, unlike those levied in the criminal courts, should be structured to impose heavier fines for delays in making repairs. Scheduled fines should also consider the severity and number of the infractions, and the number of times the owner has been requested by the local housing authority to make the repairs.

Actions to collect penalties levied by an administrative tribunal should be brought in a civil court which can obtain jurisdiction over the building (if the landlord cannot be located), with service made by mail. The trial of the issue may be directed soon after the plea is made. With rents due on most property, judgment liens could be collected more easily if normal collection techniques fail. Provisions also could be made for injunctive relief, and the city could be empowered to collect expenses out of rents for repair, vacation or demolition of buildings.

The administrative agency charged with the responsibility of housing-code enforcement should be granted investigatory and subpoena powers. The failure to register with this agency buildings containing more than three or four dwelling units could be penalized by law by either a fine or forfeiture of the right to collect rents while the building is unregistered. The establishment of such an administrative tribunal would likely result in the remedying of defects in many, if not most, instances without the need of levying or collecting fines.

I am not proposing a formal blueprint of an alternative to the present inefficient and costly method of housing-code enforcement.

I suggest that there are enough interesting possibilities available to move ahead now and appoint working committees to draft such blueprints. Even if one such alternative were established as a pilot project to be assessed by other cities, we would be on the threshold of imaginative change, as we appear to be in the area of traffic law enforcement.

OTHER ALTERNATIVES

Planning for administrative alternatives should include all municipal-code violations presently heard in criminal courts. The new concern with air and water pollution, important as it is, should not result in an expansion of responsibilities for the agencies trying to deal with street crime. The five-dollar fines imposed by the criminal courts on air polluters have not deterred continued pollution of the air by these companies. As in the case of building-code violations these fines have been considered part of the cost of doing business.

Health-code violations could be handled more expeditiously, more fairly and with less inconvenience to the public within an administrative agency. Violations of health codes result in fines. Whether it is a charge of failing to cover garbage receptacles or permitting a dog to be unleashed or dirt to collect in a yard or sidewalk, there are only two basic questions presented. The first is whether there is sufficient evidence of the charge; the second is how large a fine will be imposed. And, indeed, fines are appropriate for these violations. Most fines levied in criminal courts are low (and probably should be higher). Even the occasional case that demands a high fine, as in one decided in New York City where a large food chain was fined $7,500 for filthy conditions on its baking premises,[2] could be handled by an administrative agency. Every day in New York City cases concerning a variety of municipal-code violations are being brought in courtrooms staffed with judges, court reporters, uniformed court officers and clerks trained to process serious criminal cases. Many of these cases could be brought before nonjudicial hearing officers assigned to existing departments of government. When a homeowner leaves building material on the public sidewalk, when a street peddler fails to have a current license, when a landlord fails to remove ice from his sidewalk in the winter, when an employer fails to pay wages due his employees, there is no reason to burden those courts, struggling as they are with so many serious criminal cases.

The development of alternative forums need not be limited to cases presently in the criminal courts. The diversion of certain civil cases now heard in the courts would also make available courtrooms and judicial and nonjudicial personnel for the processing of criminal cases. This would be accomplished in jurisdictions where there is centralized control of civil and criminal courts; civil-court personnel could be trained, and, with some relatively minor renovations for the temporary incarceration of detained defendants, courtrooms could be converted to process criminal cases. If most automobile personal-injury cases (comprising over one third of the caseload in many courts) are removed from the civil courts by the advent of no-fault insurance coverage which compensates for injuries regardless of who has been negligent, there will be a substantial reduction in civil-court caseloads, and many more judges and courtrooms will be available to handle criminal cases. Similarly, if we removed tax certiorari proceedings, which provide the means for court review of the assessment of real estate taxes, or condemnation proceedings, which essentially leave for judges the determination as to the value of property taken by government, we would have additional resources for criminal cases. In all instances, the right of judicial review would remain, but the transfer of the present functions of the courts in these areas to alternative forums would make available considerable resources.

IV REDEFINITION OF CRIMES: THE ENFORCEMENT OF MORALS

To this point we have examined certain forms of human behavior which require some degree of regulation or involvement by government, although they do not reflect the gravity of serious criminal conduct. Misuse of automobiles, for example, calls for restrictions in the public interest, and alcohol and drug abuse place upon the government a responsibility to provide appropriate care. None of this conduct *must* be the subject of criminal prosecution, but all of it requires some form of action by government.

The term "crimes without victims" has been used to identify a range of criminal acts which neither cause nor threaten harm to others. Some of these involve offenses which rarely are enforced and, accordingly, represent only a small fraction of the total number of arrests and prosecutions. Others are enforced regularly, and together they represent a significant portion of prosecutions brought in the nation's lower criminal courts.

The laws proscribing illegal although voluntary transactions for strongly demanded goods and services cause the most perplexing problems for the agencies of criminal justice. These laws—outlawing homosexuality, prostitution, abortion, gambling, obscenity, and narcotics possession—are difficult to enforce because none of the parties to the transactions considers himself a victim. To offset the lack of cooperative witnesses, the police often use clandestine and highly questionable methods to gather evidence. The observation has been made that it is in the enforcement of these crimes more than any others that the courts encounter unscrupulous undercover agents, illegal arrests, unreasonable searches and seizures, and the use of electronic eavesdropping equipment. Investigating these crimes can motivate police to employ practices which, if legal, are certainly distasteful and lead to corruption and unequal enforcement of the law.

Any proposal for the revamping of our criminal laws should be viewed in the context of contemporary conditions and problems. The serious crime problem in our nation today and the inability of our criminal-justice system to respond effectively compel us to reexamine what we presently choose to define as criminal. Time devoted to the enforcement of these laws by police, courts and corrections personnel is time which cannot be made available for the apprehension, conviction, rehabilitation and fair treatment of serious criminal offenders. With the limited resources given to the agencies of criminal justice we must begin making some pragmatic judgments concerning their allocation. Professor Packer has expressed this view with conciseness and clarity:

> We cannot have all the things we want, crime prevention included. . . . [E]very trivial, imaginary, or otherwise dubious crime that is removed from the list of criminal offenses represents the freeing of substantial resources to deal more effectively with the high-priority needs of the criminal-justice system.[1]

Analysis of these crimes of alleged immorality reveals some of the high costs we pay for their retention, the ineffectiveness of the law in deterring the prohibited conduct, and, indeed, the lack of any consensus that under contemporary standards the conduct is immoral.

SEX OFFENSES

Criminal sanctions are used in almost every American jurisdiction to regulate certain sexual conduct between consenting adults. Such sanctions seek to punish what are common as well as those considered to be unnatural sex acts, and the outlawing of so-called "deviant" sexual practices applies to married as well as to unmarried couples.

The outstanding feature of these laws is that they are unenforced, and one shudders to think what it would take from our civil liberties to make them enforceable. And if they were enforced, and all guilty parties placed in jail, according to the highly publicized Kinsey reports some years ago, there would be many more Americans inside jail than outside. There is widespread disregard of laws purporting to punish homosexuality, adultery and fornication; and in the latter two cases our present ethical codes are so divided on the issue that it can hardly be said that violators—at least male violators—are held in low esteem.

A major reason for retaining these laws is the fear that repeal would be construed as a sign of governmental approval of the underlying behavior. But, on balance, what is the message communicated by widespread and open nonobservance of the law? It is paradoxical that some of the same people who cry out against disrespect for law resist attempts to conform the law to modern-day standards.

Labeling adult consensual homosexuality as criminal represents the legislation of private morality. Homosexual practices are condemned by law in forty-nine states, often at the risk of ten- to fifteen-year terms of imprisonment. Limited attempts are made to enforce these laws, and available evidence indicates that harassment of known homosexuals is widespread. Because of the difficulty of enforcing these laws, police methods raise more serious questions of immorality than the unlawful conduct itself. Acting as decoys, suggestively dressed policemen lure homosexuals into making criminal solicitations and then arrest them for violating the law.

Another traditional method of enforcing these laws is to station police "peeping Toms" in public restrooms. These unsavory and wasteful practices degrade the police officer and the public office he holds, and create the potential for blackmail by some unscrupulous people sworn to uphold the law.

The laws barring heterosexual and homosexual practices lead to some of the most pronounced instances of discriminatory law enforcement. Clear infractions may be disregarded, as in the case of the adulterous spouse who acknowledges guilt to obtain a divorce; while the real motivations for the occasional selection of persons for arrest and prosecution may not be reflected in the actual charge levied. Prosecutions on fornication charges, for example, have been brought against mothers of illegitimate children who have applied for public-welfare assistance. The press reported not long ago that the mother and father of an illegitimate child were given substantial jail sentences in New Jersey—six months for the mother and one month for the father—after an application for welfare had been made.[2] The New Jersey Supreme Court reversed the convictions but rejected the contention that the law was an unconstitutional infringement on privacy.[3]

Prosecuting the offense of prostitution presents similar problems—degrading police practices, discriminatory enforcement, harassment, entrapment and corruption—as well as the additional one, at least in New York City, of being a substantial drain on the resources of police, courts and short-term penal institutions. Besides, prostitutes, more than any other category of sexual offender, are often rounded up in street-cleaning operations without substantial evidence, in utter disregard of their rights. New York City courts are flooded with prosecutions against suspected prostitutes for loitering, solicitation and prostitution. Even the offense of jaywalking has been used to remove prostitutes from the streets.

The rationale behind prostitution laws—or at least their enforcement—extends beyond the question of morality. The male customers of these girls are virtually never arrested and in some jurisdiction are not even punishable under the law. (The Women's

Liberation movement has already voiced opposition to this clear evidence of the law's double standard.)

Other concerns in the enforcement of prostitution laws are the spread of venereal disease, the public nuisance involved, and the more serious crimes sometimes committed by prostitutes and their pimps. Free medical examinations and treatment would do more than our present procedure to prevent the spread of venereal diseases. Some prostitutes plying their trade on the streets employ an aggressive approach which is offensive to many people and is a growing source of irritation. Revised laws directed against certain forms of obnoxious solicitation would be a welcome relief to the variety of laws used today to arrest suspected prostitutes. And since many of these girls are driven to a life of prostitution by the need to pay for their drug habits, a drug maintenance program would do more than the continual dragnet arrests to reduce the number of prostitutes walking the streets of our cities.

Violence by streetwalkers is not a new development, despite published suggestions to the contrary. The criminal records of many streetwalking prostitutes are interspersed with convictions for robbery and assault. In some instances customers are lured to a remote place and mugged by the prostitute and her pimp. It is precisely because protection is needed against violent crimes and venereal disease that legalized prostitution should command serious consideration. It may well be that public sentiment against prostitution is based on attitudes toward non-marital sex relations, but this hardly ranks in importance with the need to regulate the trade to protect customers of prostitutes and the women themselves.

In some parts of Nevada prostitution has been expressly legalized, with favorable results. A well-known house of prostitution in Storey County, Nevada, affords proper screening devices to protect both prostitutes and their patrons. Narcotics are prohibited, regular medical examinations are provided, and crimes of violence are reportedly nonexistent.[4] Extending this practice to the large cities would also eliminate the public solicitation which many people find objectionable and would result in a saving of police and court efforts in enforcing the law.

ABORTION

Of the estimated one million abortions performed each year in this country, two thirds are performed on married women, and prior to their recent legalization in certain states only eight to ten thousand took place legally in hospital settings. Many of the others are either self-induced or performed under the crudest conditions imaginable by unlicensed and often untrained abortionists. Under proper conditions an abortion is a relatively safe and simple operation, but under conditions caused by the legal restrictions it is a dangerous experience, taking thousands of women's lives each year. Illegal abortion is the largest single cause of maternal death.

Several states have recently enacted legislation authorizing abortions where childbirth would pose a risk to the woman's physical or mental health. The most liberal abortion law in the country took effect in July 1970 in New York State, permitting women, residents and nonresidents of the state alike, to have medical abortions within twenty-four weeks of conception. During the first year the law was in effect some two hundred thousand women received legal abortions in New York State, and a remarkably small number, fourteen, resulted in the death of women patients.[5] The death rate is three times higher for women who give birth to children. In the last few months of the first year, during a period with the largest number of abortions, there were no deaths among the women who had legal abortions.

There is evidence that the number of illegal abortions has decreased since abortions were legalized. The maternal mortality rate dropped to less than half of what it was the year before. New York City hospitals have reported that they have treated substantially fewer victims of abortions than they did in the past. Also for the first time in ten years illegitimate births have declined.

While the moral issue concerning the right of the fetus to live is not likely to be resolved within the near future, it is obvious that other jurisdictions will closely observe the New York experience during the next year or two. The point at which the fetus obtains legal rights is not altogether clear, but one cannot help but be impressed by the pregnant woman's argument that at early stages of her pregnancy, the decision to have an abortion is a private matter which is not a proper subject for governmental concern.

GAMBLING

Arrests for gambling appear each year on the FBI's list of the ten largest arrest categories in the nation. Varying widely, the laws govern friendly wagers, weekly poker games and, in many instances, church-sponsored bingo games.

Since it is as American as apple pie, gambling has not been curbed by either the letter or the spirit of the law. It has been estimated, in fact, that fifty million adult Americans participate in some form of syndicated or professional gambling, all of which reportedly yield to organized crime an annual profit of six to seven billion dollars.[6] Gambling is said to be this country's largest and most profitable illegal industry. Gambling laws create a virtual monopoly for organized crime, permitting the huge profits to be marshaled for other—legal and illegal—enterprises, and for the corruption of public officials at every level of government.

Attempts to break gambling syndicates by imposing the harsh penalties of the law have been notable failures. As we have observed in connection with narcotics sales, the financial rewards are sufficiently high to lure enough people to work for the syndicate at any echelon, despite periodic crackdowns by police and courts. As in the cases of other consensual transactions, the police must rely on their own detection methods to arrest professional gamblers. Few people appear in police precincts to report the existence of illegal gambling establishments.

The relatively large number of arrests each year for gambling offenses do not occur without the expenditure of substantial resources and efforts by the nation's police forces. The investment of police and other law-enforcement-agency time for this offense, as with other offenses with an incidence of a large number of arrests, adversely affects the effort to control serious criminality.

The futility of enforcing gambling laws is shown in a statement released by New York County District Attorney Frank S. Hogan concerning a study of forty-seven gambling convictions during a one-month period in 1968. All but one of the forty-seven convicted defendants received small fines, which totaled $5,600. The cost of investigating and prosecuting these gambling cases was $229,000.[7]

New York City, motivated by the high revenue potential, has opened a gambling operation which seeks to compete with organized crime in off-track betting and plans to expand its coverage to various sporting events. If it succeeds it will cut sharply into the gambling operations of organized crime and eventually could obviate any need to arrest and prosecute bookmakers and "numbers" runners.

An indication that government-sponsored gambling can have an impact on organized crime is seen from recent news reports concerning the New Jersey lottery. Police in New Jersey report that the success of the state lottery has dealt a sharp blow to numbers racketeers, whose business reportedly has declined as much as sixty percent. Things are getting so bad that to compensate for the reduced profits the racketeers have felt obliged to reduce the payoff on winning numbers. The traditional payoff of 600 to one was trimmed to 450 to one. This in itself has prompted players to turn to the state lottery.[8]

OBSCENITY

Obscenity prosecutions are few and, consequently, do not result in huge allocations of law-enforcement resources and manpower.

On the other hand, those obscenity prosecutions that are brought in court cost the system much more than their small number would indicate. A substantial effort by police, prosecutors and judges may go into the trial of an obscenity case.

The writer, the director and the cast of an off-Broadway play were prosecuted on obscenity and lewdness charges recently in New York City. The matter was investigated and sent to a grand jury, which heard evidence and returned a fifty-four-count information. After an expensive five-week trial, before a three-judge bench, the defendants were convicted. One defendant paid a one-thousand-dollar fine, another paid five hundred dollars; the rest received suspended sentences.[9]

The President's Commission on Obscenity and Pornography, created by Congress in 1967 to conduct a two-million-dollar study of the effects of pornography in the United States, issued a report in September 1970. Finding that there is "no evidence that exposure to or use of explicit sexual materials play a significant role in the causation of social or individual harms such as crime, delinquency, sexual or nonsexual deviancy or severe emotional disturbances," the Commission recommended repeal of all laws "prohibiting the sale, exhibition, or distribution of sexual materials to consenting adults." [10] The only obscenity laws found to be needed were those designed to protect children from sexually explicit "pictorial material" and to protect the public from the uninvited thrusting upon it of such material through public displays or unsolicited mail advertisements.

The Commission noted that there has been a reduction in sex offenses in Denmark since legal prohibitions on obscenity were abolished in 1967. It was also reported that case studies of sex offenders in the United States showed no connection between erotic material and crime. In fact, sex offenders were found to have "sexually repressive family backgrounds, immature and inadequate sexual histories and rigid and conservative attitudes concerning sexuality."

Individual published statements of Commission members ranged from one extreme to the other. Two sociologists on the Commission urged the repeal of all laws concerned with obscenity and pornography, even those dealing with distribution of materials to children. Three commissioners wrote bitter dissenting opinions, attacking the integrity of the staff and the accuracy of the studies undertaken. The dissent did not question the lack of any established relationship between pornography and antisocial or criminal behavior. It saw as the real purpose of pornography laws the prevention of "moral corruption." The dissenters maintained that "pornography has an eroding effect on society, on public morality, on respect for human worth, on attitudes toward family love, on culture."

The Commission sent its report to President Nixon and to the Congress. The President repudiated it.

The results of this study have been circulated and every state ought to give it most serious consideration. We also ought to undertake similar studies in other areas of "morals" offenses. Such studies might put to rest some of the shibboleths relied on to retain these laws, and would provide a firmer basis upon which to take necessary legislative action.

MARIJUANA AND OTHER SOFT DRUGS

The debate continues over the dangers of marijuana and other "soft" drugs, although in recent years there has been a noticeable abandonment of some of the rigid attitudes toward their use. At this point there is no firm evidence that the use of marijuana leads to aggressive, antisocial behavior as once believed. Because it is conceivable that further studies now being undertaken by the National Institute of Mental Health may reveal long-range dangers of chronic use, it is appropriate for the government to restrict their distribution.

Punishing individuals for possessing these drugs for their own use, however, raises altogether different questions. When we convict and possibly imprison people for possessing these drugs we are in effect saying, "These products are bad for your health; we must punish you for using them." More than one person has raised the analogous health problems in the use of cigarettes and alcohol. Here is the greatest inconsistency in the message we attempt to convey in the anti-marijuana laws. Are people placed in jail for smoking, for overeating, or for consuming high-cholesterol foods or a product containing cyclamates? Government has every right, even every obligation, to attempt to convince people not to use products which are or may be deleterious to health. Licensing regulations may properly be imposed; distribution of commodities may be limited, even curtailed. But with the dearth of reliable scientific or medical data, one is hard-pressed to recall any basis or any responsible legal theory for directing the criminal sanction to the possession of small amounts of marijuana.

A recent study by the federal government revealed that one third of college students at one time or another use marijuana. A study undertaken by the New York State Narcotics Addiction Control Commission found that nearly one and a half million residents of New York State have used this drug.[11] Are we not undermining the credibility and effectiveness of the criminal law by making so many otherwise law-abiding citizens criminals?

The major rationale for the present laws is that marijuana leads to heroin. The only proof of this steppingstone theory is that many heroin addicts used marijuana at one time or another. But it would appear that most marijuana users have not graduated to the use of heroin.

The laws in force today are in need of overhaul. Uniform legislation adopted by many states punishes the possession of marijuana with a mandatory minimum jail sentence of five years. In most states marijuana is classified as a narcotic. Maximum sentences range from seven days in one state to life imprisonment in another. In practice, however, rarely is the possession of soft drugs actually punished by long jail sentences, although, to be sure, five- and ten-year jail sentences for marijuana users have been rendered. Because the possession of small quantities of marijuana can be so severely punished by law and because so many middle-class, noncriminal types of people are using the drug, prosecutors are performing legal acrobatics to find ways of making fair disposition of cases. Charges are being dismissed, reduced or held in abeyance. Convictions which are obtained are almost always for either petty offenses or, at most, misdemeanors. Many law-enforcement officials and prosecutors recognize the severity of these laws and, parenthetically, favor reclassification of possession of small amounts of these drugs into less serious categories. Reclassification has also been recommended by the President's Advisory Commission on Narcotic and Drug Abuse (1963), the National Crime Commission (1967) and the National Commission on the Causes and Prevention of Violence (1969).

Dr. James L. Goddard, former director of the United States Food and Drug Administration, has observed, "Our laws governing marijuana are a mixture of bad science and poor understanding of the role of law as a deterrent force. They are unenforceable, excessively severe, scientifically incorrect and revealing of our ignorance of human behavior." [12] Dr. Stanley F. Yolles, former director of the National Institute of Mental Health, testifying before a Congressional committee in 1969, stated that penalties "are strict enough to ruin the life of a first-time offender, with total disregard for medical and scientific evidence of the properties of the drug or its effects." He added, "I know of no clearer instance in which the punishment for an infraction of the law is more harmful than the crime."

The National Commission on Marijuana and Drug Abuse was formed by an act of Congress in October 1970. The Commission has set as its first priority the study of the enforcement of marijuana laws and is expected to report on this subject in March 1972. President Nixon has stated publicly that he will ignore any Commission proposal to legalize marijuana.

V DIVERSION OF CERTAIN DEFENDANTS

We have considered groups or categories of cases which might be better processed in forums other than the criminal courts or not be processed at all. Removing cases from the criminal-justice system may also be accomplished by diverting individual defendants charged with categories of crimes which may belong in the courts. Traditionally, when it has appeared that criminal conviction would be unduly severe, charges against some defendants have been dismissed or have been held in abeyance pending successful "adjustment" or participation in some sort of rehabilitative or similar program. Middle-class defendants fare reasonably well under this informal system. Dismissals in "the interests of justice," generally upon request of the prosecution, often are intended to preserve promising careers by avoiding the stigma of criminal conviction. The classical case for this type of dismissal in the courts today involves a college student arrested for possessing small quantities of marijuana.

The broad discretion exercised by prosecutors, in requesting dismissal of charges or permitting pleas of guilty to lesser included offenses, is not unaccompanied by problems. Acting to preserve promising careers raises serious constitutional questions (in that it results in discriminatory enforcement of law) and may lead to a system in which only the middle class is exempt from prosecution. Also, whenever informal discretion is exercised there are apt to be abuses, and, as might be expected, the individual exercising discretion is often influenced by his own background and personal beliefs. But rather than withdraw this discretionary power from the prosecutor, we should formalize alternatives to prosecution, making the exercise of discretion more visible, and offering the poor as well as the middle class the prospect of one or more of these alternatives to prosecution.

With the establishment of several kinds of programs offering specialized services, defendants charged with committing a variety of serious criminal acts would be given one or more alternatives to prosecution. Successful completion of the program in some cases would lead to dismissal of charges; in other cases in which the charges are only minor infractions of law, acceptance in the program in and of itself would be sufficient to have charges dismissed.

The development of alternatives to prosecution is an outgrowth and expansion of the traditional exercise of discretion by the prosecutor where sufficient evidence to convict is available but where, because of any of several circumstances, criminal conviction is inappropriate. By developing program alternatives to prosecution in many nonviolent cases, we would again be preserving and strengthening the criminal sanction for serious criminality and, in all likelihood, would be providing better rehabilitative services for the offenders in nonserious cases accepted in the programs.

The Youth Counsel Bureau of the City of New York provides social and job counseling to youths referred by the police, the courts and other agencies. The bulk of its caseload is comprised of youths placed on long-term parole by the Criminal Court of the City of New York soon after charges are levied. Cases referred in this manner are adjourned for a period of three to six months, during which time the youths selected for the program are placed under supervision and given guidance and assistance by Bureau staff. Youths under the age of twenty-one who have not been previously convicted and who are not charged with serious crimes qualify for this program. Following a "favorable adjustment" over a period of three to six months, a case referred to the Youth Counsel Bureau will be dismissed in court. Nearly ninety percent of youths referred by the courts on long-term parole show favorable adjustments during these periods. It is unrealistic to believe that any significant degree of rehabilitation takes place in so short a time after arrest, while charges are still pending against these youths, but the value of the program is obvious. Aside from removing a few thousand cases each year from the courts' congested calendars (some 6,300 in 1970), and relieving defendants of the stigma and the attendant employment disabilities of criminal conviction, the prospects of rehabilitation in these cases are at least as good before as they are after conviction.

Another diversion program, called pre-indictment probation, was begun in January 1971 in Philadelphia. The district attorney's office screens all serious nonviolent offenses involving defendants with either minimal or no criminal histories. Defendants selected from the screening process are advised of their rights and, if they agree to the terms of the program, are given informal and unrecorded hearings. Nothing said by the defendants at the hearings can be used against them. Thus, it is conceivable that a defendant may admit his guilt at such a hearing and later, if deemed unacceptable for the program, deny his guilt on trial—and not be challenged with his earlier version.

The victims in the cases selected for hearing are invited to participate in person or by expressing their views in writing. The court considers all of the evidence, including the defendant's background, to determine solely whether he poses a threat to the community. If the court and the prosecutor agree that the defendant is a good risk, charges are deferred for six months, a year or more. If he maintains a clean record during this probationary period, charges against him are eventually dismissed. If he fails to remain out of trouble the original charges are reinstated. At no point is he placed on formal probation; he is simply given a chance to mend his ways. Selected drug users are referred to a voluntary agency which, after appropriate medical examination and diagnosis, makes further referral to various narcotics treatment facilities throughout the city. Representatives of the voluntary narcotics referral agency, and of other community agencies, are assigned to the courtroom where the informal hearings take place.

During the first six months of the Philadelphia experiment slightly more than twenty percent of the felony cases were selected for hearings. Approximately eighty percent of these—some thirteen hundred cases—were approved by the court and the prosecutor for the program. During this period changes were made in the categories of cases selected for hearings. Serious assault cases had not been ruled out early in the program, because of the hope that with the passage of time complainants and defendants would mend their differences. When this did not transpire in many of the cases, such categories of crime were no longer screened out for hearings. A similar cutback was made in nonviolent gun-possession cases, because of the growing gun problem in Philadelphia. On the other hand, more serious cases were accepted when it appeared that there was some infirmity in the prosecution's case—such as inability to justify the search undertaken by the police.

Officials in Philadelphia regard the experiment as a success. They see the need for an expanded rehabilitative staff, linking professionals and volunteers, and are seeking Safe Streets Act funds for this purpose. A new program is being planned, for the added reason that a change in the jurisdictional responsibilities of the courts has recently moved most of the less serious felony cases to the (lower) Municipal Court.

A New York City program similarly intended to divert people charged with traditional criminal behavior is the Manhattan Court Employment Project, which is specifically designed to assist the poor man charged with crime. Persons charged with extremely serious felonies are not considered for the program. Also unacceptable are full-time students, middle-class defendants who are apt not to repeat criminal behavior, and people earning adequate salaries—all of whom are unlikely to be benefited by an employment program. Of the first 850 participants in the program, over eighty percent were black or Puerto Rican.

The Manhattan program attempts to provide counseling and employment to people in need of these services. Staff counselors are from the slums and have had firsthand experience with deviant behavior, most having served prison terms themselves. They have limited caseloads and are able to devote adequate time to the people within the program. Close relationships with private industry have been established, and reasonably well-paying jobs are secured for participants in the program. Repeated attempts are made where necessary to place participants in industry. What distinguishes the Court Employment Project is that it is not middle-class oriented. Initial failure strengthens the resolve of staff to achieve ultimate success. All employers are asked to cooperate with the program's goals by being tolerant, at least initially, of a limited amount of lateness and absenteeism. This is not to suggest that rejection of the entire program by participants will be tolerated. The staff knows that its credibility in the courts is the only sound basis for continuation and possible expansion.

After a defendant has been selected for the program and agrees to participate, a ninety-day adjournment is secured in court. On the adjourned date, a project representative makes one of three recommendations: (1) renewal of the prosecution, (2) dismissal of the charges, or (3) a second adjournment to give staff more time to work with the defendant. In more than half of the cases, prosecutions have been renewed because the project staff has concluded that its continued services would be of no value. This large rate of failure is explained by the relatively large number of heroin addicts who have unintentionally been taken into the program. It is a fact in New York City that perhaps half of all defendants arrested for crimes are addicted to heroin. A concerted effort is made to exclude addicts from the program, because their needs simply cannot be met with basic counseling and employment services alone.

A program similar to the Manhattan Court Employment Project is the Washington, D.C., Project Crossroads, which accepts youths between the ages of sixteen and twenty-six who have charges pending against them in either criminal or juvenile court. Every participant is assigned a trained, nonprofessional counselor who is responsible for providing supportive services and for submitting evaluation reports to the appropriate court. The counselors maintain close contact with the participants assigned to them. Daily meetings are held at the beginning of the program, and counselors are expected to meet with participants at their homes, on their jobs and in their neighborhoods. The heart of the plan is employment and vocational training; remedial education is also provided for youths placed on jobs or in school.

As of September 1970, of the 750 participants who had completed the program, the cases of 517—representing fifty-five percent of the enrolled juveniles and seventy-seven percent of the enrolled adults—were favorably terminated, and charges against them were dismissed. A fifteen-month follow-up study was made of two hundred adult participants who had completed the program. A companion group of defendants normally processed through the courts was also studied for that period of time. The program participants who favorably completed the program had a recidivism rate (the term is used loosely, since it is based upon arrest only) of 22.2 percent during the fifteen-month follow-up period. The control group had a 45.7 percent recidivism rate—twice as many.

Diverting youths accused of deviant and other criminal behavior has been a traditional part of the nation's juvenile-court systems, and a brief assessment of these procedures provides interesting models for use in the criminal-justice systems. It has been estimated that about half of all accused juveniles are not processed through the courts. Both the police and various types of court "intake" personnel combine to divert many of the cases which might otherwise be pursued. The rationale of this policy is to give young people who have manifested some deviancy "another chance." It is puzzling why giving another chance to people who have committed illegal acts should be limited arbitrarily to youths under the age of sixteen or eighteen and be unavailable to older persons who show promise of being able to lead useful lives in the future. While it may be necessary to draw arbitrary age lines to determine who shall and who shall not be treated as juveniles, youthful offenders and adults, we should take notice of the fact that adult maturity is not exclusively a feature of adulthood, and, conversely, that immaturity is not exclusively limited to youths.

The Office of Probation in the New York City Family Court staffs an intake service with the explicit function to meet with complainants and respondents and "adjust" cases which need not be processed to trial. Similar screening procedures exist in most juvenile courts. The existence of these intake procedures reflects a legislative policy to release prior to any trial or dispositional hearing some youths who do not require the assistance of the courts. If this policy is advisable for juveniles, there is no reason why it should not be applied to older youths and adults.

Another program designed to divert youths from the juvenile courts, and provide services to keep them out of trouble, is being tried in a poverty section of New York City. The Neighborhood Youth Diversion Project, sponsored by the Vera Institute of Justice, relies on neighborhood aides, trained by professionals, to bring to bear on a youth's problems the social services already available in the community. Also, new services are being developed under the program. The aides carry small caseloads to ensure that sufficient individual attention is devoted to the youths assigned to them. They maintain responsibility over their cases even if referrals are made to existing social-service agencies.

A Work Detail program which permits certain youths to secure dismissal of charges was instituted in a small suburb of Detroit and has been adopted in other areas. These youths, who have either no previous criminal records or minor ones, agree to work for the city for a full year. Ninety-eight percent of those who have been assigned to the program in Royal Oak, Michigan, have successfully completed it. Clearly, this concept has merit. A defendant with some potential for rehabilitation is permitted to avoid the stigma of a criminal conviction, while at the same time engaging in some service to the public.

The National Crime Commission recommended the establishment of a neighborhood agency to provide comprehensive counseling services for juveniles who could be referred to it by the courts prior to the dispositional hearing stage. This agency would coordinate all of the services available in the community and would develop services not presently being provided by any existing agency. Curiously, the well-considered materials on avoiding court processing and adjudications for juveniles were not made applicable by the Crime Commission to adult cases. The establishment of such a comprehensive treatment agency should be an equally important part of the adult criminal-justice system. Conviction of juveniles or adults should not be required in every case in order to make rehabilitative services available, particularly in view of the extremely high rate of failure of correctional processes after conviction. The only proviso which must be stressed is that in any system, whether juvenile or adult, the alternative to prosecution must be voluntary and the rights of participants must be protected in every way.

At a time when the vocal public is demanding more and even harsher laws, it is increasingly more difficult to repeal repressive legislation. The development of alternatives to prosecution provides some balance against the harshness of criminal sanctions and permits some siphoning of the multitudes of cases confronting the agencies of criminal justice. New screening devices should be used in the courts to identify defendants who should not be prosecuted instead of relying on the current haphazard exercise of this discretion. All cases should be screened, not just those that defense counsel bring to the attention of prosecutors with requests for special handling. Prosecutors should take the lead in requesting dismissal of cases where more appropriate alternatives exist or where it is clear that evidence of guilt beyond a reasonable doubt is lacking.

In 1967, as part of an experiment to keep an arraignment court operating beyond the normal eight-hour working day in New York City, we gave to the district attorney of New York County a responsibility unprecedented in that jurisdiction. He was charged with drawing the complaint in every case and thereby rejecting at very early stages in criminal proceedings cases in which evidence was lacking. The result today is that twenty thousand cases each year are dismissed within hours of arrest. Twenty thousand defendants who had been arrested earlier by the police and then brought to court for arraignment are freed prior to arraignment. This procedure should be expanded to embrace the services of probation personnel who know of the availability of alternative programs and the wide range of existing social agencies. A strengthened screening unit would weed out all cases unworthy of prosecution—on social as well as legal grounds.

PART TWO

IMPROVING THE NATION'S CRIMINAL-JUSTICE SYSTEMS

VI AN OVERVIEW OF THE SYSTEM

All agencies playing a role in the arrest (police), adjudication and sentence (courts, prosecution and defense), imprisonment (pre- and post-conviction detention), or supervision (probation and parole) of persons accused or convicted of crime are part of our criminal-justice system.

The thousands of local criminal-justice systems in this country have in common, in addition to their goals, the same basic procedures. Thus, following arrest, a suspect is brought to court for the ultimate purpose of determining whether there is sufficient evidence to establish his guilt. If such evidence is lacking, the case is dismissed and no punishment or regulation is imposed upon the defendant. If guilt is established by the evidence, and the defendant is found guilty, the court may impose upon him certain restrictions. He may be sentenced to serve a prison term, the most severe of these restrictions; or he may be released outright on a suspended sentence; or he may be released but placed on probation and required to meet certain specific obligations imposed by the terms of the sentence and to report regularly to an assigned probation officer.

A simplified diagram shows how a case travels through the three basic components of the system.

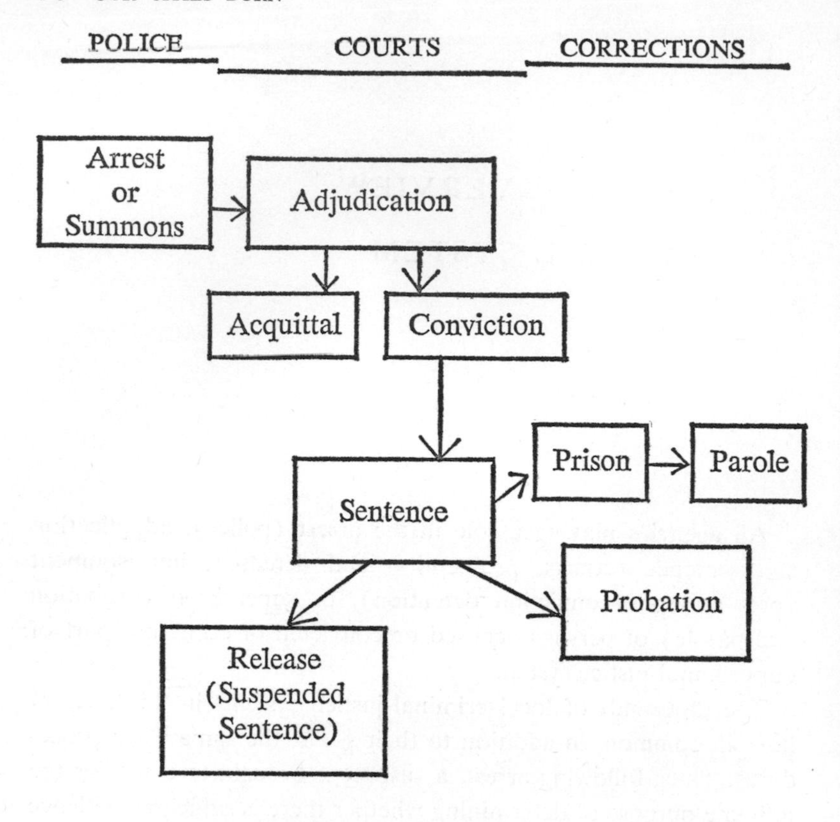

A more sophisticated analysis would show the many component parts of the system from arrest through corrections. Most defendants are brought into the system through an exercise of judgment by the police that reasonable grounds exist to believe that one or more criminal laws have been violated. A police officer may see a crime committed in his presence or may witness enough to give him cause to believe a crime is being committed or has been committed. The latter situation may arise, for example, when a police officer hears a scream and sees somebody lying in the street and a suspicious person running from the scene. Often witnesses observe the commission of a crime and report their observations to the police, sometimes pointing to suspects. All of these situations lead to arrests by the police. Less frequently, the police make arrests authorized by warrants signed by judges who have been satisfied that there are reasonable grounds (called probable cause) to believe that the persons named in the warrants have committed crimes.

Following arrest the defendant is brought to a police precinct, and if a superior officer on duty agrees with the judgment of the arresting officer, the defendant is "booked" (certain information is recorded) and fingerprinted (in all but some nonserious cases). He may then be questioned, photographed and held for appearance in court before a magistrate. In some jurisdictions defendants charged with less serious crimes may be released from the precinct and directed to return to court on a future date. Release from the precinct in some jurisdictions is conditioned on the posting of collateral (generally a bail bond, obtained from a surety) which is subject to forfeiture in the event of failure to appear in court. In other jurisdictions, those who seem more likely to return to court are given summonses at the discretion of the police and released. Generally, all defendants charged with serious crimes are taken to court following processing by the police.

The time between arrest and the first appearance in court (known as arraignment) varies from jurisdiction to jurisdiction, and from case to case. If a defendant is arrested either after or near the end of the court session for that particular day, he may be detained by the police until the following morning. If he is arrested on a Saturday afternoon in a jurisdiction which has no arraignment court in session on Sundays, he may be detained for nearly two days by the police. On the other hand, if he is arrested early enough on a day that court is in session, there will be minimal delay between his arrest and his first court appearance.

In most cities arraignment courts are in session during the hours of a normal working day. Occasionally, a judge in a small or medium-size city will arraign a defendant after court hours at the request of defense counsel. In New York City an arraignment court is in session sixteen hours of every day in the week.

When an arrested person appears in court on the first appearance, he is advised of the charges lodged against him and of his rights which accrue at that stage. In some jurisdictions all defendants, except those charged with traffic offenses, are advised of their right to counsel. This explanation should refer to the right to the free services of counsel for defendants who are unable to afford these services. In other jurisdictions, only those defendants charged with serious crimes are given free counsel, and hence are advised of this right. When defendants appear with counsel at this early stage the "reading of the rights and charges" is usually waived at the request or with the approval of counsel. Except in very serious cases such as murder, bail is fixed or the defendant is released on his own recognizance (pretrial parole) without any provisions for furnishing bail or collateral.

One of the purposes of the initial appearance in court is for the magistrate to conduct a preliminary hearing to ascertain whether there is sufficient evidence against the defendant to justify continuing the prosecution. Frequently, this hearing is not held on the first appearance because the parties are not prepared to proceed or because the judge, faced with a large calendar of cases, simply lacks the time to hear the testimony of witnesses. In a sizable number of cases this hearing is waived by defendants.

The first proceeding usually takes place in a court with summary jurisdiction—that is, power to try cases to conclusion and determine guilt or innocence—over only the less serious criminal matters; these comprise misdemeanors (punishable by a prison term of one year or less) and petty offenses (punishable by a shorter term such as fifteen, thirty or sixty days). It processes more serious cases up to a point, but can dispose with finality of none but misdemeanors and petty offenses. Since this court (it may be called a municipal court, district court, police court, magistrate's court or criminal court) has no final jurisdiction over felonies—the more serious offenses, punishable by more than one year in prison—it cannot accept either guilty or not-guilty pleas in these cases. On the other hand, since it has final jurisdiction over less serious offenses, the magistrate presiding requests defendants charged with such offenses to enter pleas of guilty or not guilty.

A plea of not guilty sets into motion a sequence of events leading to a trial unless, of course, there is a guilty plea entered sometime prior to, or during, trial. Once a guilty plea is entered the only question remaining is the type of sentence to be rendered.

At the first court appearance, if the case has not been disposed of by dismissal or plea of guilty (trials are almost never held on the first appearance in court) it is adjourned and scheduled for another appearance. Felony cases generally are scheduled for preliminary hearings and are subsequently bound over for action by the grand jury unless charges are dismissed or reduced to misdemeanors, in which event they are handled to completion by the lower court.

The grand jury is a forum of persons (more than the twelve that usually constitute petit juries during trial) which determines in felony cases whether there is sufficient evidence to warrant a trial. In some jurisdictions the grand-jury procedure may be waived, and the case then proceeds directly to trial. There is no right to counsel in a grand-jury proceeding. The judge presiding is not present. Defendants are not called to testify unless they make specific request to relate their side of the story to the grand jurors. If a majority of grand jurors vote in favor of proceeding against the defendant after hearing the evidence presented by the prosecutor, an indictment is drawn charging the defendant with a crime. The grand jury may also vote to dismiss charges or reduce felonies to misdemeanors for further proceedings in the lower court. Felony trials are held in courts of general jurisdiction, often called superior court.

Initial processing prior to trial takes from several weeks to several months. In more serious cases such as rape or homicide, it may take up to two years and occasionally, in some overcrowded courts, three years before a trial is commenced. The extent of the delay is caused by a variety of factors, including the number of pretrial motions brought by defendants. In recent years the courts have expanded procedural rights of defendants and, consequently, have increased the number of pretrial challenges that can be initiated. Another factor in the delay of cases is the size of caseloads; in large urban areas, where crime is more prevalent, there are more cases to process and, hence, greater delays in moving cases to trial. In some cases delays are caused by the parties: the prosecution and, more often, the defense seek long and repeated adjournments to suit their own ends.

There are several points prior to trial within the court process at which disposition may be made of the charges. In a fairly substantial proportion of cases—as much as thirty to forty percent in some jurisdictions—charges are dismissed. This can occur at any stage of the proceeding prior to conviction. There follow some illustrations of cases dismissed on motion of the prosecution.

1. Prior to the initial appearance before the magistrate the prosecutor assigned to the court reviews the evidence and discovers that there is insufficient evidence to convict a defendant. The prosecutor requests a dismissal of the charges or effects a dismissal by his failure to file charges with the court.

2. Following a hearing on a motion brought by the defendant, critical evidence is suppressed after a judge concludes that it had been obtained in violation of the defendant's constitutional right against unreasonable searches; or a confession vital to the prosecution's case is held to be involuntary and obtained illegally. Lacking sufficient evidence to introduce at a trial, the prosecutor requests a dismissal of the charges.

3. In preparing a case for trial, a prosecutor determines he has a weak case for one or more reasons: a key witness has died or disappeared, or his witnesses will not stand up against cross examination in court. He requests a dismissal.

Most cases—in fact the overwhelming number—do not go to trial. Either they are dismissed prior to trial or, as is generally the case, a plea of guilty is entered to a lesser or reduced charge. Perhaps the most criticized and least understood part of a criminal prosecution concerns the plea of guilty and the so-called deal which precedes it. The process by which these pleas are arranged is often referred to as plea bargaining, a term which relates to the negotiations which take place between the prosecution and the defense counsel, sometimes the judge, for a mutually acceptable plea. Obviously, the defense counsel, in relieving the state of the obligation to bring the defendant to trial, attempts to secure a plea to a charge less serious than the one originally lodged. He seeks the least serious charge he can obtain for his client, while the prosecutor seeks to obtain a plea which would most closely reflect the actual crime committed. A more elaborate description of this process is deferred until later; it is sufficient at this point to observe two important reasons for plea bargaining. There simply are not sufficient facilities or manpower to bring to trial all or even half or a third of all cases. Unless some enticement is held out to defendants there is no reason for them to plead guilty; they might just as well go to trial if their only alternative is to plead to the original charges.

Of the millions of criminal cases instituted each year in the nation's courts, relatively few—perhaps three or four percent—proceed through trial. The right to trial by jury is guaranteed by the United States Constitution. The United States Supreme Court recently held that this right extends to all persons charged with crimes punishable by prison terms of more than six months.[1] In many jurisdictions even defendants charged with petty offenses have the right by state law to jury trial. Some defendants choose to waive their right to jury trial and elect instead to be tried by a judge.

On the trial of a case, the prosecution has the burden of establishing the defendant's guilt beyond a reasonable doubt. If the trier of the facts—the jury or, if a jury trial has been waived, the judge —has a reasonable doubt after all the evidence is heard as to whether the defendant is guilty, an acquittal must follow. In a jury trial a decision of acquittal or conviction must be unanimous. Any split vote results in a mistrial—in which case the defendant may be retried. Thus, if eleven jurors vote to convict and any juror votes to acquit, a mistrial will ensue. Conversely, if eleven jurors vote to acquit and one juror votes to convict, the defendant may be brought to trial again.

Under the system of law in operation in this country there is great concern for the rights of defendants. A heavy burden of proof is imposed on the prosecution. In a civil case a verdict is granted in favor of the party who has established his case by a preponderance of the evidence. But in a criminal case the prosecution should not secure a conviction merely because it has submitted somewhat more credible evidence than was presented by the defendant. It must prove guilt beyond a reasonable doubt.

The defendant in a criminal case cannot be compelled to testify; he may choose to remain silent, to not take the stand, and to present no evidence at all. No comment may be made by the prosecution as to the defendant's silence; and no inference of guilt may be drawn from defendant's silence by the jury.

The prosecutor's burden in establishing the defendant's guilt has been compounded by a series of high-court decisions which have been rendered over the past several years. Evidence in the possession of the prosecution tending to exculpate the defendant must be made available although a corollary burden is not placed upon the defendant to give the prosecution evidence of his guilt. Moreover, not all evidence may be used by the prosecution. If physical evidence is seized from the defendant in violation of the right against unreasonable searches and seizures, it cannot be used against him. Incriminating statements made by the defendant to the police may be excluded from the trial if the police violated the defendant's rights at the time they questioned him. Thus, if they denied him his right to counsel or failed to advise him of his right to have counsel made available, any incriminating statement made by the defendant will be excluded from the trial. Similarly, if the defendant is not advised, before being questioned, of his right to remain silent, or if he indicates in any manner that he chooses not to respond to police questioning, any subsequent statement taken in which he explicitly or implicitly reveals his culpability will not be admissible against him on the trial of the case.

Abusive practices throughout the years have constrained the courts to make the kind of rulings described in the preceding paragraph. The establishment of guilt is not the only end to be served by the administration of criminal laws. The police and the prosecution must also abide by the law. Since there seems to be no practical remedy against police abuses other than to exclude evidence wrongfully obtained, the courts have taken these steps.

In balancing the rights of defendants against the need to gather and present evidence of crimes, the courts have had a difficult role to play. If the control of crime were to become an overriding concern of the courts it is entirely conceivable that we would lose many of the freedoms we hold so dear. Because we believe, for example, that the conviction of an innocent person is the extreme injustice—more insupportable than the failure to convict a guilty person—the system reflects this value. In establishing the rules by which evidence of criminality is gathered and used we must maintain sufficient protection for the accused, even at the cost of making it difficult to arrest and convict people, and even at the cost of letting some guilty persons go free.

Several years ago, before the courts put a stop to the practice, it was not unusual for the police to arrest people on the slightest suspicion, without reasonable grounds to believe that they committed crimes. Annual arrest reports published by the Federal Bureau of Investigation listed "suspicion" arrests for some police departments; and in certain cities more than half the arrests made for serious crimes were not brought to court. For many people suspicion arrests meant inconvenience, embarrassment and false accusation.

Suspicion arrests also have been made under false charges of vagrancy or public intoxication. When the police wanted to hold suspects for questioning or while they checked some leads they sometimes booked the accused under trumped-up charges. It was not unusual for a person to be charged with a petty offense, held for several hours in a police station, and then booked for a more serious crime or—more often—released because intensive police questioning failed to link him with the crime.

Many years ago it was frequent practice to use excessive force on suspects being interrogated; this practice apparently is not so widespread today, although many charges of beating are still made by suspects. In recent years the style of interrogators has changed. As the United States Supreme Court recently noted, "interrogation is psychologically rather than physically oriented." [2]

Police interrogation became an art designed to elicit confessions. False promises and lies were an integral part of the interrogator's arsenal. Police manuals were published describing a variety of questionable methods which could be employed to get suspects to confess.

The "Mutt and Jeff" ploy, as described in the manuals, called for a tough, relentless officer and a friendly, sympathetic one. Mutt, the tough officer, would play his role first—impatient, threatening, intolerant. Then Jeff, the kindhearted officer, would speak to the defendant. As one of the most popular police manuals describes his role:

> He has a family himself. He has a brother who was involved in a scrape like this. He disapproves of Mutt and his tactics and will arrange to get him off the case if the subject will cooperate. He can't hold Mutt off for very long. The subject would be wise to make a quick decision . . . When Jeff makes his plea for cooperation, Mutt is not present in the room.[3]

The manuals used by the police offer other interrogation alternatives:

> The accused is placed in a line-up, but this time he is identified by several fictitious witnesses or victims who associated him with different offenses. It is expected that the subject will become desperate and confess to the offense under investigation in order to escape from the false accusations.[4]

The manuals advise interrogators how to respond to requests by suspects to talk to counsel or to their refusal to answer questions. The suggestion is made in clever terms that such requests suggest guilt. Interrogators are also advised to deprive suspects "of every psychological advantage." [5] The interrogation, they are told, should never take place in surroundings familiar to the suspect, where "he may be confident, indignant, or recalcitrant" and where he "is more keenly aware of his rights." [6] The unfamiliar, hostile environment of the police station is considered basic to fruitful interrogation.

Over the years, the rights of suspects in police stations have been enlarged by court decisions which cracked down on brutal practices. The 1966 Supreme Court decision in *Miranda v. Arizona*[7] mandating that suspects be advised of their rights was the outcome of decades of abuse in police precinct houses. It gave meaning to the constitutional rights previously enjoyed mostly by experienced and hardened criminals who knew about them.

Similar meaning was given in 1961 to the right of freedom from unreasonable searches and seizures. The law traditionally has permitted searches of people, their homes and their businesses only when the police had probable cause to believe that the suspect, the target of the search, engaged in criminal conduct. Prior to 1961 the right to be free from unreasonable searches was meaningless. We all had this right without means to insist that it be obeyed. The police would search people, and break into their homes without the required knowledge, without ever having received approval from the courts, without search warrants, and any evidence seized would be used in court. People whose rights were violated had no grounds to protest. In 1961, the United States Supreme Court in *Mapp v. Ohio*[8] gave us all greater protection by ruling that illegally seized evidence could not be used in local and state courts against defendants whose rights had been violated.

Despite Supreme Court decisions, the police still at times flagrantly violate the law, and the courts must continually be called upon to reassert the rights of citizens. In Baltimore during a nineteen-day period in December 1964 and January 1965 the police conducted searches of more than three hundred houses in an area inhabited mostly by blacks, in an effort to capture Samuel and Earl Veney, two brothers who had killed one policeman and wounded another. Without search warrants, acting on unverified, anonymous tips from unknown persons, the police entered private dwellings carrying shotguns, submachine guns, tear-gas apparatus and bullet-proof vests. Adults and children were awakened in the middle of the night by flashlights shining in their faces. The searches were fruitless.

It may be argued that there was a genuine purpose in conducting these searches; certainly it was in the public interest to apprehend the Veney brothers. But what price must be paid in terms of our basic liberties to permit such an unauthorized police response to crime? A United States Court of Appeals ruled in this case that the police should be enjoined by the courts from future searches in the absence of probable cause. The language of the court is instructive:

> In ordering the issuance of an injunction, we have not blotted from our consideration the serious problems faced by the law enforcement officer in his daily work. His training stresses the techniques of the prevention of crime and the apprehension of criminals, and what seems to him to be the logical and practical means to solve a crime or to arrest a suspect may turn out to be a deprivation of another's constitutional rights. And where one policeman is killed and another wounded, the police, and the public too, are understandably outraged and impatient with any obstacle in the search for the murderer. While fully appreciating the exceedingly difficult task of the policeman, a court must not be deterred from protecting rights secured to all by the Constitution.
>
> The police department is society's instrumentality to maintain law and order, and to be fully effective it must have public confidence and cooperation. Confidence can exist only if it is generally recognized that the department uses its enforcement procedures with in-

tegrity and zeal, according to law and without resort to oppressive measures. Law observance by the police cannot be divorced from law enforcement. When official conduct feeds a sense of injustice, raises barriers between the department and segments of the community, and breeds disrespect for the law, the difficulties of law enforcement are multiplied.[9]

Protection of the innocent, even apart from high-court decisions, sometimes makes it difficult to convict the guilty. Occasionally there is no other choice. Not long ago, the body of a young woman was found on a deserted road in a rural part of Michigan. She had been abducted, raped and murdered. A witness saw one of twin brothers leaving the scene of the crime, but he could not identify which one of the twins he had seen. Both brothers were arrested. Subsequently, charges were reluctantly dismissed by a judge who commented that one of the two brothers had committed the horrible crimes but there was no proof as to which was the culprit.[10]

The temptation exists to take the easy way out—to curtail the rights of citizens, to make it easier for the police to make arrests and gather evidence. The Attorney General of the United States recently decried our "preoccupation" with defendants' rights. We *should* be preoccupied with rights—and they are the rights of all citizens—and we should cling to the freedoms which our laws and our courts have made available to us.

VII THE POLICE: THE FOCUS OF ATTENTION

Police occupy the front line in the nation's efforts to control crime. They patrol the streets, investigate complaints of crime, and attempt to apprehend people suspected of committing criminal acts. There is a great deal we do not know about the relationship of these functions to crime on the streets, but there is basis for the belief that enhancing efficiency in police performance of these functions has some bearing on the amount and the type of crime which is committed. A few years ago the disturbing rise of crime in New York City subways was stemmed by a massive increase of police assigned to the subways. It appears that criminals became convinced of the substantially greater risks involved in committing crimes in the subway. Whether they chose other occupations or shifted the site of their unlawful endeavors we just do not know.

Despite the dearth of hard data, we can assume that some criminal acts will not take place if we can substantially increase the likelihood that perpetrators of crime will be arrested. It is hardly probable that criminals know what the precise police "clearance" rate is, or know that only one serious crime in fifteen or twenty results in a conviction. But it is not unlikely that criminals, or at least some of them, have a sense of the inherent risks involved in committing certain crimes and would refrain from criminal activities if there were a reasonable certainty that they would be arrested and convicted.

Making the police more efficient has increasingly become a major concern of government over the past few years. A range of improvements in police management, administration and investigation was recommended in 1967 by the National Crime Commission, and it appears that with the infusion of federal (Safe Streets Act) funds some efforts are being made in this direction. Computerized communications systems, for example, are being developed in a few jurisdictions to enable the police to respond to calls for assistance in a fraction of the time it takes with equipment available in most other cities. There has also been experimentation with computerized retrieval systems, which permit the almost immediate retrieval of information deposited in what systems analysts call a master file of stored data. One application of this data-processing technique, recently perfected on a statewide basis in California, permits the police to obtain information about a particular suspect, vehicle or weapon from a master file within seconds of the request for information. The introduction of computers in California has reduced the waiting time from a minimum of one hour to seven seconds for each response to a request for information.

The National Crime Information Center in Washington, in operation since 1967, provides information by computer to law-enforcement terminals in forty-nine states and the District of Columbia. This computer has stored within it more than a half-million records on stolen motor vehicles, stolen license plates, stolen or missing guns and other articles, and "wanted" persons and can provide within seconds information requested of it. A computerized file of arrests and dispositions, presently available on a statewide basis in some areas, is being planned on a national scale by the Crime Information Center. After it is perfected police agencies in any part of the country will be able to discover for the first time whether a particular person has been arrested before in any area of the country.

A federal grant has permitted fifteen states (Arizona, California,

Colorado, Connecticut, Florida, Illinois, Maryland, Michigan, Minnesota, New Jersey, New York, Ohio, Pennsylvania, Texas, and Washington) and some federal agencies to collaborate on a massive criminal-history file of felons with at least two arrests each. These records are stored for computer retrieval through a national index operated by the Michigan State Police. The information is available to police agencies, courts and corrections personnel in any of the fifteen participating states. Similar types of electronic information systems are being developed in thirteen other states.

Computers are also being used experimentally by a few local police departments as internal-management devices. In Oakland, California, a computer gathers detailed statistical information concerning personnel and provides a variety of personnel reports which are of assistance in the assignment of police officers. Deployment of police manpower is also made in St. Louis with the help of a computer, which predicts areas in which calls for assistance are likely to occur. In addition to providing accurate and timely information, computers save hours of police time by printing a variety of reports needed by local police departments.

Federal crime-fighting funds have also encouraged studies designed to improve the effectiveness of police weapons, patrol cars and uniforms. Helicopters are used for routine patrol operations. An attempt is being made to develop a battery of psychological examinations for police applicants which could accurately predict future performance. Several types of police training programs are being funded throughout the country. And closed-circuit television systems, bringing sections of urban areas under the surveillance of the police, are being tried as anticrime devices.

A closed-circuit television surveillance mechanism in Mount Vernon, New York, caught sight recently of a man going in and out of doorways. As he explored the inside of a pizzeria he was greeted, to his surprise, by police officers dispatched to the scene by an officer on duty at the television monitor. After the suspect's arrest one officer commented, "He must be new in the area. I guess he didn't know we have those cameras." [1]

Perhaps the most fundamental crime-control reform undertaken by police and local government has been the realignment of police personnel in order to make more efficient use of available manpower and to provide greater protection on the streets. The use of police scooters is an attempt to retain the traditional notion of "walking a beat" while giving the individual officer greater mobility and enlarging the area which can be protected. Several steps are being taken to put more police officers on the streets. The most direct one—requiring additional funds—is the hiring of more policemen. In some jurisdictions civilian clerks and police trainees have replaced police officers who used to perform clerical chores. The use of specially trained tactical patrol forces represents an effort to saturate high-crime areas with additional police manpower.

In New York City, the traditional deployment of police officers into three shifts has been modified by the addition of a "fourth platoon," which is used between the hours of 6 P.M. and 2 A.M. This additional shift places more police officers on the streets during the hours when most serious crimes are committed. A similar shift was created in Washington, D.C., following a 1966 study revealing an "inefficient and unnecessary" disparity between assignments of police on patrol and the hours when most crimes occur. It seems incredible that in some of our major cities it took until the late 1960s to consider, as part of the planning for assignments, the time of day when police officers are most needed; but it is precisely because we are beginning to think in terms of management techniques to control crime that these types of basic changes are being made.

The strengthening of law-enforcement capabilities, necessary as it may be in the battle against serious crime, is not free of serious problems. There is always the danger, for example, that as an overreaction to crime the police may be given equipment which is not really relevant to street crime and which may be misused. Capitalizing on the fears produced by the civil disorders of the mid-1960s, weapons companies placed a range of new devices on the market for purchase by police agencies. Billy clubs with push-button gadgets to spray chemical gases, as well as shields, helmets and several types of tear-gas canisters, have been commonly displayed at police conventions.

The indiscriminate spraying of chemical compounds such as Mace by the police and the use of police dogs and shock-producing batons to control demonstrators have signaled the most obvious dangers of new weapons. A Presidential commission report on crime in the District of Columbia criticized the haphazard use of police dogs to patrol slum areas. The commission observed that police dogs on occasion had even bitten drunks being arrested in the Skid Row area of Washington, D.C. Ironically, the misuse of new equipment had an adverse reaction on crime-control efforts recently in Berkeley, California, where in May 1969 a National Guard helicopter had been used to spray tear gas on campus demonstrators. One year later a proposal to purchase two police helicopters was defeated by the Berkeley City Council, after a heated debate centering on the earlier experience.

A related danger in the issuance of bigger and better equipment for the police is that despite the help the additional resources offer in fighting crime there is often a threat to our right of privacy, as well as to other fundamental rights which should be exercised free from arbitrary police action. It is not difficult to understand how police-operated closed-circuit television systems can offer the ultimate in protection by permitting the streets of a city to be under the careful inspection of a police official who can summon instantaneous help by way of a computerized communications system. But neither is it difficult to comprehend why we should be apprehensive about appearing on a large television screen in the local precinct house whenever we are on the public streets—although in large cities a minor dividend might be a more scrupulous observance of local ordinances when walking dogs on sidewalks.

Although this can be an effective precaution, it can be argued that too much surveillance can seriously impair our right of privacy.

This troublesome issue is also raised by the accumulation of data through modern computer techniques. While the need for data exists at various points within the criminal-justice system, the recent acknowledgment by several police departments and by the United States Department of Justice and the United States Army that detailed files are kept on citizens who participate in public demonstrations, and even on public officeholders sympathetic to the politically unpopular, indicates that the development of more efficient ways to maintain data may also be a threat to the enjoyment of basic rights.

A federal court recently banned the surveillance of and collection of dossiers on people who did nothing more than exercise their constitutional rights of free speech and assembly in opposition to the war in Vietnam.[2] And the Philadelphia Police Department, which has boasted of its dossier collection, has agreed to terminate the practice of asking people arrested for antiwar activity political questions concerning associates, organizations and so-called subversive sentiments. The agreement to terminate this practice was a condition of terminating a lawsuit brought by the American Civil Liberties Union in federal court. The ACLU had contended that the questions were not relevant to the crimes charged and were designed to stifle free speech.

Perhaps the clearest threat to privacy in the name of crime control is the development of highly sophisticated electronic surveillance equipment. Professor Allan V. Westin of Columbia University Law School in his book *Privacy and Freedom*[3] catalogues the terrifying potential of existing listening devices, including microphones which can, through the use of laser beams and radar, pick up from miles away objects in a room. News stories a few years ago warned of the installation of minute microphones in martini olives. (If, as it has been reported, wiretapping has discouraged the use of telephones by men in organized crime, it may be that when conspirators now meet they also ask their hosts not to serve martinis.)

The Administrative Office of the United States Courts reports that state and federal judges granted all of the 597 applications made in 1970 to engage in wiretapping. From these 597 requests there resulted telephone taps of 390,000 conversations.[4] The major purpose of these telephone taps was to gather evidence on people suspected of being engaged in gambling and narcotics crimes. More than half of the 390,000 intercepted conversations bore no implications of criminality.

No information is available on wiretaps performed without judicial approval for what is called national-security purposes. The questionable legality of this practice is presently being litigated, and it is expected that the United States Supreme Court will rule on it in the near future.

One of the important questions raised by wiretapping and electronic surveillance is whether the results obtained are worth the price we pay for this type of governmental snooping. There are only certain crimes which lend themselves to this type of investigation. When a tap is placed on the telephone of a suspected bookmaker it does not distinguish among his incriminating and nonincriminating telephone calls. Nor does it turn off when his children or his wife use the telephone. We can never be certain, until after conviction, that the suspicions of the law-enforcement authorities will be confirmed. The suspect may, after all, be innocent. The problem of invasion of privacy is aggravated when a tap is placed on a public telephone. In a celebrated Supreme Court case taps had been placed on the public telephones of a bar and grill and certainly had picked up conversations of innocent people.[5] A famous lawyer has told of a case in which a tap on a public telephone intercepted conversations between husbands and wives, lawyers and clients, physicians and patients. He reported that "the most intimate details of these people's lives became a matter of police record as the result of a single wiretap." [6] In another of his cases, an electronic device placed in a hotel room recorded conversations between a man and his wife.

In a sense, the dangers in the development of new equipment are similarly presented by the placing of large numbers of additional policemen on the streets. While the need for protection on the street is obvious there comes a time when too much police coverage just raises the prospect of having stricter enforcement of the myriad petty offenses which even the most law-abiding of people may commit at one time or another. A study taken in Washington, D.C., a few years ago, established that the majority of arrests made by a newly established tactical patrol force was for the crime of public drunkenness. The President's Commission on Crime in the District of Columbia found that it was "boredom," the need "to find something to break the monotony" [7] of routine patrol, that caused the tactical force to make drunkenness arrests. A similar expansion of a tactical patrol force's responsibilities occurred in New York City. These specially chosen police officers have been engaged for years in the city's attempt to fight serious crime. Recently, their duties have been extended to the arrest of prostitutes.

The warning sounded here about the potential dangers in giving the police too large a share of the available crime-control funds is not intended to suggest that improvements in police techniques and equipment are unnecessary or inadvisable. To the contrary, some of the improved techniques are unquestionably necessary, but two caveats must be sounded about them. First, they must be carefully and periodically reviewed. Background data and criminal histories must by law be kept confidential and unavailable in most instances even to public agencies outside the criminal-justice system. Second, if funds must be rationed among several agencies we must guard against going overboard in providing police with equipment and manpower, the funding for which might be more intelligently diverted to agencies functioning in the subsequent stages of the criminal-justice system, where the needs are at least as compelling.

Local governments have given the police the bulk of funds devoted to crime control—as much as eighty percent, according to the most recent statistics available in New York City. Federal crime-fighting funds made available through the Safe Streets Act have also been primarily devoted to helping the police, under the original Law Enforcement Assistance Program of the Department of Justice. Of the $20.6 million distributed between 1965 and 1967, only $50,000 was provided for the courts.[8] And, while some improvement has been shown by the current program, a marked pattern of favoritism for police projects, by the federal government as well as by the states, continues to exist. During fiscal year 1969, only three fourths of $1 million was given to the courts, for example, out of a total of $25 million distributed.[9] At the present time the Department of Justice claims that eleven percent of the total (Safe Streets Act) funds is given to the courts, but this includes a substantial amount for prosecution and defense agencies.

The National Urban Coalition has recently published a report criticizing the use of federal crime-control funds. The Coalition found that there has been a "broad dissipation of action funds" which has resulted in the money "not being focused on major impact programs" and having "little likelihood of preventing or reducing crime." Moreover, said the Coalition, the money in some cases "is not going to the urban population centers—where the crime is." The Coalition also concluded: "Almost all of the 1969 action money went for police expenditures—usually communications equipment or other hardware—while only negligible attention was given to such areas as corrections, juvenile treatment, narcotics control, or court reform." [10]

A recent news item related the expenditure of $61,000 in federal funds to teach policemen in Texas to understand Spanish. Ordinarily this would be a worthwhile effort to establish better relations with Spanish-speaking people. But some question concerning the wisdom of the grant is raised by a reported quote from an institute spokesman: "The officers must know the cuss words so they will know when they're being insulted." [11]

Perhaps the greatest danger of focusing attention on the police in the nation's effort to control crime is that we tend to overlook the rest of the criminal-justice system—oversights which create imbalances in its functioning. Improving the chances of apprehending suspected criminals, while an imperative initial step for an efficient criminal-justice system, does not give us an effective and impartial adjudication process or a correctional process which does more than provide storage under conditions as intolerable and outdated today as they were fifty years ago.

Moreover, and this is the greatest irony of all, enlarging and improving a police force only make it more difficult for the rest of the system to function. More police result in more arrests and more business for the court and the correctional processes, already dreadfully overburdened. It is simply no answer just to arrest more people. Without a well-funded and smoothly functioning system of criminal justice they will be turned back to the streets, innocent and guilty alike, often more knowledgeable in the ways of crime than before they were arrested. An arrest gives the system an opportunity to identify a person's needs and, where appropriate, to rehabilitate him. Unless we understand the limitations of the police function and its role within a larger system we will never make any headway in solving the growing crime problem. And governmental efforts over the past few years have shown little realization of these factors.

Enhancing police efficiency is not the only improvement in law enforcement which can help in the nation's war against crime. Through more capable leadership the police must become less isolated, less arrest-oriented and, generally, more a part of the mainstream of intelligent crime-control efforts.

All too often the police have been identified with a single response to crime—the hard-line approach which is critical of permissiveness in court decisions, "coddling" of criminals, and any attempt to restrain their powers. There are approximately forty thousand local police forces in this country, employing more than 420,000 people. Among these are all types, representing a variety of views. Some believe that the solution to the crime problem is in a strengthened police effort. Others, perhaps less vocal, appear to have recognized the complexities of crime and the need for a broader, more progressive approach. New innovative programs have gained police support. For example, few police officials have spoken in favor of continuing the futile practice of arresting public inebriates. They do not want the job and, for the most part, they support new treatment techniques. The first detoxification center in operation in this country was a project sponsored by the St. Louis Police Department. It applied for and received federal funds in 1966 for the care of homeless inebriates in a building that had been previously used as a hospital. Under that program inebriates are brought to a detoxification center where they remain for seven days and receive the type of care provided in the Manhattan Bowery Project described in Chapter II.

The New York City Police Department has given its fullest cooperation to the efforts of the Vera Institute of Justice to achieve reform in the criminal-justice system. One example is the Manhattan Summons Project, begun in 1964 and subsequently extended to all counties in the city of New York and adopted by other cities. Under this project, now operated by the police in New York City, each year some 30,000 people believed to be good risks to appear voluntarily in court are given summonses in lieu of arrest. They are taken to the precinct houses and permitted to leave with summonses instructing them to return to court at a specified time. This procedure saves these defendants the ignominy and inconvenience of post-booking procedures and several hours—and what was often an entire night—of detention. The courts are aided by having fewer cases clogging arraignment parts. The cases are scheduled for advance dates when they may be processed more conveniently by the courts.

During the past two decades a great deal has been said and done about police professionalization—raising standards of police work and improving operations and training. One of the results of this concern has been to promote higher education, both as a threshold prerequisite for the position of police officer and for purposes of advancement within the police ranks. Criticism has been leveled at the police for failing to emphasize, as part of the concern for professionalization, good relations with people in the communities being policed. It has been pointed out, and substantiated by reliable studies, that police practices have engendered hostility and hatred on the part of minority groups toward the police.

There have been some attempts in recent years to develop better police–community relations. Placing community residents in New York City police precinct houses as receptionists and training them to handle social problems are valid efforts toward developing better relations with residents. The assignment of several full-time police officers in San Francisco to help youths with police records find jobs is another commendable police effort.

Studies by the National Crime Commission suggest that much more needs to be done in this area. Existing police community-relations personnel were found to have little support from ranking police officials.[12] It was also found that too often the police efforts were not aimed to reach the young and the disenchanted. Other Commission studies pinpointed an unfortunate lack of community-relations units within police departments. Observers traveling in patrol cars with the police in Chicago, Washington and Boston painted a picture of physical abuse, surliness and bigotry.[13] They found that in fourteen percent of contacts with victims, witnesses and defendants in cases involving suspected crime the police employed abusive language. Widespread physical abuse was also witnessed. And it is important to note that these instances of physical and verbal abuse occurred in the presence of Commission observers. It is a fair surmise that the problem is more serious in the absence of official observers. A large number of the white officers who were accompanied by observers expressed prejudiced remarks concerning blacks.[14] Racial bigotry on the part of police was confirmed by a recent federally funded study of the Miami, Florida, department; it was reported that police routinely made disparaging references to blacks, and that the principal animosity by police was toward teenagers and young adults in the black community.[15]

These studies, in the light of the well-known vocal hostility expressed on the part of minority groups toward police, reflect the need to improve police–community relations. Attempts must be made within police departments to change negative attitudes through better training devices, to take greater precaution in utilizing the higher salaries now paid to attract more capable and tolerant candidates for police work, and to enlarge and support police community-relations units.

In a society rocked by attempts to take policemen's lives, and where respect for law and order is a battle cry of politicians and policemen alike, greater efforts also must be made to reduce what has been described as widespread police corruption. The National Crime Commission reported that its studies revealed "a significant number of officers engaged in varying forms of criminal and unethical conduct." [16] According to a published report in the New York *Times,* Commission observers reported that they had seen some police officers whom they accompanied seek and accept unlawful gratuities.[17] A special commission investigating corruption in New York City reported recently the same pattern—widespread police corruption at most levels of the department.[18] Police were found to be taking money from drug pushers, prostitutes, after-hours liquor clubs, bookmakers, and a broad range of businessmen.

Much of this corruption occurs in the slum areas. Slum residents know when the police are on the "take." Their children know it. One of the laudable efforts being made in the slums today is seeking to set new models for slum youth—away from the slick hustler who relies on grabbing the fast buck, and toward the more conscientious, highly motivated person who achieves success and status through legitimate means. The policeman can be a positive model for slum youth. But before that can happen great strides must be taken to reduce substantially the disturbing proportion of corruption we are told exists in the ranks of the police in certain communities.

VIII THE COURTS

There is no single description of courts common to all communities. In some areas there are new courthouses with a sufficient number of courtrooms and related facilities. In other areas proceedings take place in grimy, fortresslike buildings. Shortages of courtrooms sometimes compel the use of converted office space and judges' chambers for hearings and trials. In these instances handcuffed defendants are taken through public corridors to get from a detention area to a courtroom. In the New York County Criminal Court Building a number of trials are regularly held in judges' robing rooms, because of a shortage of formal courtrooms. From time to time the court reporter must raise his hand to silence a witness whom he cannot hear because the toilet in the adjoining lavatory is being flushed.

Court proceedings also take place in police precinct houses and city halls; justices of the peace in rural areas sit in American Legion halls, in private offices and in the rear of retail stores. Other differences prevail. Some judges are experienced in the criminal law, others are not; some are not even lawyers. Also, the nature of cases varies. The lower criminal courts in areas where crime is prevalent are faced with more serious cases than courts in rural areas.

In some cities, court proceedings are informal; defendants are brought before judges who follow few of the formalities prescribed by statute or by state and federal constitutions. Often when proceedings are informal defendants are not represented by counsel and there is no record taken of what is said in court. In other areas proceedings are recorded and defense counsel play an important role; basic procedural laws are followed, as are the strict rules governing the type of questions which may be asked during hearings and trials and the type of sworn testimony which may be given.

Variations also exist in the hours of court. In most jurisdictions arraignment courts shut down at 5 P.M. Until about five years ago, anyone arrested in New York City after 2 P.M. could not be arraigned in Criminal Court that same day. The processes of conveying the defendant to the station house, booking him, fingerprinting him, taking him to Police Headquarters for identification checks, and drawing the complaint in the courthouse consumed several hours and could not be concluded before court had recessed for the day. Moreover, the arraignment of a large number of defendants during a limited number of hours created a scene matched only by the city's crowded subway system during rush hours.

Many of us regarded these conditions as intolerable, so we launched in the Criminal Court, experimentally in one county at the outset, the twenty-four-hour arraignment program. Three sessions of court were instituted, including the existing one, which commenced at 9 A.M. and ended at 5 P.M. A second session under the new program began at 6 P.M. and ended at 1 A.M., and a third ran from 2 A.M. to 8 A.M.

For six months the arraignment court in Manhattan was open around the clock. Due to shortages in personnel and other resources, the experiment presented serious difficulties for the agencies that staffed the courts—the district attorney's office, the Legal Aid Society, the Departments of Correction, Probation and Police, and the courts themselves (judges, clerks, court officers, court reporters, interpreters). Many of the people on the 2–8 A.M. ("lobster") shift found it difficult to withstand the rigors of working those unusual hours.

After the initial six-month experimental period it became obvious that the strain imposed on the limited number of personnel was too severe to continue the full program. It was equally clear, however, that the program resulted in a more even distribution of cases and alleviated much of the chaos which had previously existed. Also, most of the defendants arrested after 2 P.M., who had been able to secure their release, were not compelled to remain incarcerated overnight. The decision was made to continue the program in a modified version. The 2–8 A.M. shift was eliminated, leaving an arraignment court in operation until 1 A.M. every day of the week.

There was one unexpected dividend from the new program. We could not muster enough complaint clerks to man all three sessions; their important function requires a high degree of experience, intelligence, and a certain mastery of the criminal law. District Attorney Frank S. Hogan cooperated by supplying assistant district attorneys to staff the complaint room. Prior to this experiment there had never been prearraignment screening of complaints by the district attorneys' offices. The decision to arrest, made usually by police, had been, in effect, a decision to prosecute, and the court clerks would not ordinarily overrule it. Cases deemed unworthy of prosecution were dismissed at stages of proceedings subsequent to the drawing of the complaints, often after three or more adjournments.

The impact of placing prosecutors in the complaint room to review all cases prior to arraignment was salutary. The prosecutor assigned to the complaint room makes the decision whether to proceed in the first instance. If he believes that the arrest should not have been made or, for any reason, that the prosecution should not proceed, he simply does not bring it before the court. This procedure, which arose out of the twenty-four-hour arraignment experiment, renders invaluable assistance to a court deluged with cases.

In large urban centers, cases scheduled for a particular day are placed on "calendars" and are called in rotation. Witnesses are expected to be in court early in the morning and to wait for the calling of the cases in which they have a role. It is common for the same cases to be called more than once because of the absence of witnesses, defendants or attorneys. Witnesses and defendants who appear on time, especially in large city courts, often wait for several hours until some disposition is made of their cases. And the dispositions are usually not final. Adjournments more often than not are granted because the cases are not ready to proceed. Four or five adjournments in each case are common before final dispositon, and sometimes fifteen to twenty and even more adjournments are granted. This means that before any affirmative action is taken, witnesses frequently are required to appear in court on many occasions. As a result, some complainants, in sheer disgust, refuse to cooperate with the prosecution and, consequently, cases against guilty defendants must be dismissed for lack of evidence.

The harassed judges presiding over these overburdened court sessions called "calendar parts" in large cities have done little more than press the attorneys to proceed and then, when either the prosecution or the defense is not ready, grant adjournments. The primary purpose of calendar parts is to assign cases ready for judicial action to "back-up parts," which are available for hearings and trials. In some cities, judges in calendar parts handle their own hearings and trials—often following the completion of the calling of the calendar.

The large volume of business in metropolitan courts has led to an overriding concern with speed in the handling of cases. Getting through the day's cases seems uppermost in the minds of the judges presiding and their staffs of court clerks, attendants and reporters. Some judges in the New York City Criminal Court—the court conducting preliminary hearings for felonies, and trials and summary dispositions of misdemeanors and lesser crimes—contend that there is barely enough time in the day even to adjourn knowledgeably all of the 200 to 250 cases on each of the calendars. Hundreds of people are packed into courtrooms, standing in the aisles and corridors.

Largely because of the emphasis on speed, there is a substantial deviation, to say the least, between the textbook model of due process and what actually takes place in court. In cities where prosecutors' offices are not sufficiently staffed to cover the lower criminal courts, police officers—often the arresting officers—present the facts, cross-examine witnesses and make references to the law in their legal arguments to the judge presiding in court. One recent study noted that when police officers act as prosecutors the presiding judge, instead of listening to the evidence in his impartial, judicial role, plays an active part in eliciting testimony.

Flagrant abuses occur periodically in the wake of civil disorders when the need arises to process unusually large numbers of cases. It is under conditions of stress that a system's weaknesses are exposed most graphically. A great deal of understanding, therefore, can be gleaned from a study of how the system works under crisis conditions and can be profitably applied in the day-to-day operation of the courts.

In riot situations large-scale arrests are followed by large-scale arraignments, temporary detention in crowded, often crudely makeshift jails, and the subsequent handling in court of a few serious and many nonserious cases. During some of the 1967 riot cases, as many as a thousand defendants in one day were herded through an arraignment process. And in several jurisdictions those detained prior to the first court appearance, and held because of inability to raise high bail following arraignment, were kept in quarters without adequate space, light, or toilet facilities. Even buses were used as detention facilities in one city following the 1967 civil disorders.

When large numbers of defendants are processed in court during a limited time period, a variety of shortcuts are taken, and guaranteed procedural and due process rights are often disregarded. A series of informative articles and officially sponsored reports have been published recently detailing the abuses in the administration of criminal justice under emergency conditions.[1] When the courts have been swamped with cases, required statutory warnings have been perfunctory, and scant attention has been paid to the criteria which form the basis for bail and sentencing decisions. Mass—instead of individual—preliminary hearings have been held, and in some cases the presiding judge has denied defendants their right to confront accusers or to cross-examine adversary witnesses. Counsel has been present in name only, unable to function adequately because of the immense responsibilities imposed and the speed with which cases were moved to completion. The line between innocence and guilt often is blurred, and too many guilty pleas have resulted from the horrible conditions under which defendants have been detained. During the 1967 Detroit disorders, for example, innocent people, whose resistance had been destroyed by detention because of inability to raise high bail, pleaded guilty and received suspended sentence.

In one city, arrest reports were misplaced; and with a touching faith rarely exhibited by prosecutors in the integrity of defendants, the latter were asked to cooperate by helping to charge themselves with crime.[2] Defendants who had been detained for twenty-four hours or more were interviewed by teams of prosecutors and defense counsel who asked the defendants what they had been arrested for and what they had done. Based on the information secured from the incarcerated defendants, arrest reports were completed and charges were filed in court—literally out of the mouths of those charged.

The lesson learned from the published reports of the administration of justice following civil disorders is clear. A court process overwhelmed by cases makes its primary concern moving the calendar and disposing of cases and is proportionately less concerned with due process of law. Moreover, a hard-pressed court is less efficient and less able to identify serious offenders who require supervision in a correctional setting. It is a tragic error to dismiss these published reports as merely the symptomatic aftermath of such rare phenomena as civil disorders. While the volume problem is not as acute during ordinary times, the daily intake of cases in large-city criminal courts is far too great for proper handling with the limited resources and procedures available. In some respects the daily administration of justice in the nation's lower criminal courts is as riddled with problems as it is following mass arrests of civil-disorder defendants. The latter place in sharp relief the everyday deficiencies of the criminal-justice system.

Appropriate screening devices to weed out defendants who should not be prosecuted are rare, and most courts continue to be bogged down in the handling of a variety of innocuous petty offenses such as traffic and other local infractions which simply should not be in court.

So many cases are brought to metropolitan courts during normal times that perhaps only three or four minutes are allocated to each defendant for the all-important arraignment process. Within this period the presiding judge must advise the defendant of his rights and of the charges against him, inquire into the defendant's record and background, make a determination on pretrial confinement or release and set bail conditions where applicable. The reading of the rights and charges is often rendered by court officers who garble their words to the point of nonintelligibility. And for those defendants with less than a college education or who experience difficulty with the English language, the results are obvious. They not only fail to understand what is being said but, if they have not been through the system before, they are apt to be totally confused about the nature, scope and significance of the proceeding.

Over ten years ago, when the Vera Foundation launched the Manhattan Bail Project, which sparked bail reform throughout the nation, the difference between the way properly instructed defendants and uninstructed ones accommodated to the mysteries of criminal-justice procedures was made dramatically manifest. In the project's experimental stage, Vera personnel instructed defendants orally about returning to court and the necessity for appearing promptly, handed them reminder cards in English and Spanish, and then mailed them second reminders a few days before the adjourned date. During the Vera experimental period the nonappearance rate for defendants released on their own recognizance—without bail—averaged the astonishingly low figure of one and a half percent, much less than that of defendants released after furnishing bail. When the New York City Probation Department took over operation of the bail program, it temporarily relaxed the notification program. The nonappearance rate climbed to several times the previous ratio.

Compounding the failure of communication between the court and indigent defendants is the frequent lack of satisfactory legal representation. Because public-defender agencies are overwhelmed with cases, sufficient time and individual attention are not available for each client. Often there is no rapport between the indigent defendant and his attorney or a succession of attorneys from the same public defender or legal-aid office among whom he is shuttled; consequently, and understandably, the defendant has little faith that he will be justly treated.

Adequate representation means careful preparation, investigation, interviewing of witnesses, consultation with experts in certain cases, and the utilization of lawyerlike skills learned through formal training and experience in court. Even the most capable trial counsel cannot perform adequately without undertaking a thorough inquiry into the allegations and the likely testimony of witnesses. Proper preparation also includes candid, and often lengthy, discussions between the attorney and his client.

The National Crime Commission's report depicts the status of our nation's courts:

The commission has been shocked by what it has seen in some lower courts. It has seen cramped and noisy courtrooms, undignified and perfunctory procedures, and badly trained personnel. It has seen dedicated people who are frustrated by huge caseloads, by the lack of opportunity to examine cases carefully, and by the impossibility of devising constructive solutions to the problems of offenders. It has seen assembly line justice.[3]

Ironically, conditions are worse in many respects than they were in early 1967, when the Crime Commission was "shocked" by what it witnessed. Since 1967 there has been relatively little increase in financial assistance to build courthouses and hire more court personnel. Caseloads, however, have increased enormously since that time. There has been an increase in crime, an increase in the number of police officers, an increase in the number of arrests and, consequently, an increase in the number of prosecutions. In New York City there were 192,534 cases processed by the courts in 1967. By 1970 that number had grown to 249,126.

One of the depressing features of providing a description of the courts and their procedures is the realization that it has all been said before—to no avail. The National Crime Commission said it in 1967, and thirty-six years before that another national crime commission, the Wickersham Commission, reported the same shortcomings and abuses. A description of a big-city court as far back as the turn of the century rings true today as well:

> The trials were shameful in their lack of dignity and fairness . . . The courts were wretchedly housed in miserable and generally very noisy quarters.
>
> There were no adequate records kept, no means of determining the old from the first offenders. . . .
>
> Into these crowded, unwholesome courts every morning were drawn as in a vast net hauled from the depths of the underworld, the prostitute, the thug, the drunk, the pickpocket. . . . Together with these were herded the poor, ignorant, unfortunate violators of petty ordinances . . .[4]

Changes have occurred since the early 1900s, and many attempts have been made to improve court procedures. The descriptions of ten, twenty and even fifty years ago have nevertheless remarkable applicability to modern times because of the growing problems faced by the courts. Reform has been overridden by increasing caseloads—and this will continue to be the case unless substantial overhauling is effected.

BAIL AND PRETRIAL DETENTION

Pretrial detention presents perplexing problems in the administration of justice. Defendants, of course, are presumed innocent until proven guilty. There are some defendants, however, who appear to be poor risks to return to court to answer the charges brought against them. Are they to be released prior to trial? An issue of extraordinary difficulty facing us today is: Should a person be released pending trial if he is charged with a vicious crime and has a record of having committed violent crimes in the past?

So-called preventive detention of presumably dangerous defendants before trial is advocated by some as a preventive measure against specific conduct deemed contrary to the public interest, such as tampering with witnesses while at liberty, failing to return to answer charges, and committing crimes while awaiting court action on the pending charge. Predicting that certain people will engage in delinquent behavior is not, in itself, unfair or repugnant to constitutional norms. Defendants are placed on probation or in prison largely because, in the course of sentencing them, judges have made some prediction about their future behavior. In the case of preventive detention the underlying prediction of future delinquent behavior is implemented against defendants who have not yet been convicted of any criminal conduct. And the net effect of detaining defendants before trial is to punish them in advance of any adjudication of guilt. In jurisdictions where pretrial detention is not accompanied by speedy trials, people are deprived of their liberty for months, in some instances for years, awaiting disposition of their cases. Even the preliminary hearing, the brief judicial review of the evidence called for by law, is often postponed until after pretrial detention has begun; consequently, many defendants are detained solely on police officers' judgments that they have committed crimes.

Over ten years ago an experimental Vera project was begun in New York City to determine whether appropriate criteria could be developed to guide the court in making the critical pretrial detention decisions. The Vera Foundation was established to determine whether the courts could depend on defendants deemed to have roots in the community to reappear if they were released on their own recognizance—released on their honor. A grading system was established under which a defendant who was employed, owned property and had resided in the community for a substantial period of time would score high and one who had no ties to the community would score low. Those who scored reasonably high were considered likely to return to court; those who scored low represented greater risks. The high scorers were recommended to the court for release on their own recognizance without posting bond or other security. The low scorers were not recommended for the program; in order to obtain their release pending trial they had to raise bail or an equivalent.

The dramatic results of the experiment, demonstrating that those who were released on their own recognizance returned to court in 98.5 percent of all cases, led to a major reform in pretrial detention. Large numbers of people were released who under the earlier procedures would have been detained in jail because of inability to post security. This program or some variant of it spread to over one hundred other communities throughout the nation, where similar results were obtained.

The Vera project of a decade ago was a pioneering effort, one which I was proud to support and to assist in forming. It did not profess to offer a complete solution to the problem, but through the years it has resulted in freeing many defendants from the hardships imposed by pretrial detention.

The Des Moines, Iowa, Model Neighborhood Corrections Project, commenced in October 1970, is an attempt "to supply the equivalent of 'roots' to those who have been passed over initially for pretrial release because of their lack of stable community ties." The Des Moines Pre-Trial Release Project, implemented in 1964 and patterned after the New York City Vera experiment, has been successful. From 1964 to 1969, some 3,800 defendants have been released on their own recognizance pending disposition of their cases; of these, only 2.4 percent failed to appear for trial. The 1970 Model Neighborhood Corrections Project is designed to permit the release of those defendants who, because of lack of established community ties, do not qualify for release under the 1964 project.

Defendants released to the 1970 project must report daily to a counselor. Some are required to participate in personal, family or group counseling. In addition, they may be required to attend evening classes in alcoholism, drug abuse, employment, the use of legal counsel and welfare services, planned parenthood, medical insurance, vocational rehabilitation services or remedial education. They also may be referred to one or more of a variety of public and private agencies for such services as employment, budget planning, child-care training, drug or alcohol treatment, remedial education or vocational evaluation.

During the first eight months of the Model Neighborhood Corrections Project's operation, eighty-one defendants who had been detained in jail were released to the program, and eighty percent of these were afforded multiple services, primarily employment and psychological. Only one defendant failed to appear for trial. Five were charged with new criminal offenses during the pretrial period and were returned to jail. Based upon these preliminary results the conclusion was properly drawn that defendants released to this pretrial project who would otherwise remain in jail presented no greater risks to flee or to commit crimes while they were free than other defendants released pending trial.

The most shocking aspects of pretrial detention stem from the conditions under which defendants may be incarcerated. The nation's jails have been aptly called "brutal, filthy cesspools of crime" by a high-ranking United States Department of Justice official.[5] Heavy cinder blocks, characteristic of jails, prevent proper flow of air, and prisoners in some jurisdictions face almost intolerable heat during summer months. Vermin, cockroaches and other insects often share space with prisoners. Forced homosexuality is rampant, and brutality by prisoners and guards is a way of life in many of these institutions. Idleness prevails. A recent Department of Justice study revealed that eighty-five percent of the nation's jails have no recreational or educational facilities of any kind!" [6] Sometimes prisoners are forced to remain cramped in their cells for as many as twenty-two hours of every day. In New York City many of the approximately ten thousand prisoners sleep on bunks without mattresses. A guard in a New York City jail, expressing his views on how prisoners live, was quoted as saying, "If I were locked up, I'd be raving mad in a month." [7]

Adding to the inherent injustice of pretrial detention is the fact that defendants who are too poor to pay a bondsman the premium for bail bonds or who cannot secure release on their own recognizance remain incarcerated. Large numbers are in jail—nearly twenty percent of all those in pretrial detention in New York City—only because of their inability to post even nominal bail. Two people may be arrested for committing the same crime and, because of similar backgrounds, may be held in the same amount of bail; if one of them is able to raise the premium for a bond and the required collateral and the other is not, the first will go free pending trial while the second will languish in jail.

We need to remind ourselves every so often that at least some defendants held in overcrowded detention facilities will not be convicted of anything. Among those in pretrial detention today are some whose cases will be dismissed by the prosecution for a variety of reasons; others will be found not guilty after trial. Only recently, in New York City, two defendants held in pretrial confinement for more than two years were released at the request of the district attorney's office after their innocence was firmly established. At one point during this past year, there were four defendants detained in New York City jails for periods from eight to twenty-four months whose innocence was established by independent evidence and acknowledged by the district attorney's office.[8]

In a recent case, a man charged with armed robbery was jailed in default of five thousand dollars bail after his accuser told the court, "This is the man. I'm sure of it. I see his face in my dreams." [9] Subsequently he was cleared of the crime when it was established that at the time the crime was committed he was in jail on another charge. In another case a Washington, D.C., man positively identified a suspect as the perpetrator of a holdup. The suspect was jailed. Months later, after another man confessed to the crime, the witness looked at him and exclaimed, "My God, this man looks exactly like the other one." [10]

Injustices can occur despite all the safeguards provided by law. In one case two witnesses swore under oath that a particular defendant robbed a bank. Following his conviction and imprisonment another defendant was accused of the same crime. At his trial the same two witnesses, acknowledging their mistake in the first trial, pointed to the second defendant as the culprit.[11]

The uncertainty of identification testimony is underscored by the invariable contradictions that occur when witnesses at any time are asked to describe a complicated event. A robbery by several people of a Manhattan café not long ago resulted in a wide variety of descriptions of events to the police. The New York *Times* reported:

> Witnesses gave conflicting accounts of the holdup, apparently because of the dim lighting and movement of the holdup men and woman around the partition.
>
> One witness thought there were four in the gang, another said there were nine. Another victim said he thought that only one of the holdup men used the spray [Mace], while others were sure that most, if not all, of the robbers used sprays.[12]

In another recent case in New York City a defendant was falsely accused and detained pending trial, having been charged with selling heroin to an undercover agent. After the defendant had been in detention for five months the district attorney realized that a policeman's allegation concerning the conversation prior to the sale of the heroin was false. The defendant was a deaf mute, unable to utter intelligible sounds.[13]

Pretrial detention for more than the briefest time creates similar injustices for people who *have* violated the law. It is not uncommon for delay pending trial to be as long, or nearly as long, as the ultimate period of incarceration ordered by the sentencing judge. If a defendant is unable to post bail he may spend as much time in pretrial detention as he would in post-trial detention after conviction and sentence. Indeed, there have been cases in which defendants were incarcerated before trial for periods longer than the maximum sentences which could have been imposed after conviction. At the signing of the federal Bail Reform Act—which grew out of the New York City Vera experiment—President Johnson recalled the case of a man who could not raise three hundred dollars bail while awaiting trial on a traffic offense. The man spent fifty-four days in jail prior to trial on a charge which carried a maximum jail penalty of five days. In Maryland, a man charged with disorderly conduct was held for ten weeks because of his inability to pay a $16.60 bond premium. In New York, a woman, apparently unable to raise a twenty-dollar premium after being arrested on a narcotics charge, served twenty days until it was discovered that the alleged narcotics were merely thyroid pills. And in Detroit a man held for failure to raise a ten-thousand-dollar bond served one year in jail before being brought to trial on a charge of stealing five boxes of cookies from a grocery store.[14]

New alternatives to pretrial confinement must be developed. The District of Columbia has had favorable experience with a program of supervising defendants released pending trial. An attempt is being made in New York City to develop a similar program, in which defendants not ordinarily qualified for release on their own recognizance would be released to volunteer attorneys and community groups. In some instances, the volunteers will accompany defendants to court. This experimental procedure promises an alternative to pretrial detention. A variation of it would be to require released defendants to maintain close ties with an agency of the court, such as a probation office. Defendants could be required to report on a weekly basis, to communicate with the office either daily or two or three times a week, to keep the office advised of their whereabouts.

Compounding the pretrial-detention problem is the fact that so large a number of persons caught up in the criminal-justice system are narcotics addicts who must commit crimes daily to support their habits and are notoriously unreliable in honoring their obligations to appear in court. Release pending trial would apply to the addicts who as a group commit the large bulk of crimes—misdemeanors and nonviolent felonies. But short prison terms (before or after trial) are not a major crime-control factor. People cannot be removed from society forever, despite those who might favor it. And when their release is weighed against the injustice of pretrial detention, I have no hesitation in urging that except perhaps in extraordinary circumstances these defendants be set free pending disposition of their cases, even at the risk that some of them will disappear.

A more difficult problem is presented by the person charged with committing one or more violent crimes. When a particularly dangerous defendant is brought before the courts (this occurs relatively infrequently), his detention pending trial or pending other disposition should be brief and under humane conditions. If we cannot provide a speedy trial and, pending trial, humane detention, he too should be released.

Identifying defendants who may fairly be regarded as dangerous is the greatest weakness in the preventive-detention concept. It is likely that laws authorizing the detention of dangerous defendants will be applied to people who should be free pending the outcome of their cases. One New York City judge recently held two prostitutes without bail because of the danger he said they presented to the community. He cited the spread of venereal disease as the basis for his determination—without even having it determined whether they suffered from the illness. Congress recently passed a law authorizing preventive detention in Washington, D.C. It is certain to be tested in the courts.

The underlying problem in this area runs throughout the administration of justice: If society wants certain standards of protection, it must pay the price for a better system. Presently we force the accused to pay this price. In most communities, particularly large cities, if he is charged with a crime of violence and unable to be released pending trial, we tell him that he must remain in a small cage for several months, sometimes up to two years, because we are unable to bring him to trial sooner. Certain standards of proper treatment, however, must be met regardless of the volume of cases and government's perennial financial crises. We cannot tolerate infringements of these basic standards of fair play any more than we can tolerate other deprivation of rights in the name of necessity—such as doing away with trials or removing the burden on the prosecution to establish guilt.

Recently some courts have moved to relieve these conditions. The Second Circuit Court of Appeals, in its administrative capacity over the federal district courts within its jurisdiction, has promulgated rules setting a time limit for the disposition of cases. A maximum limit of six months after arrest has been set, within which time all cases must be ready for trial. After that period—unless the prosecution can show good reason why it is not ready for trial—untried cases will be dismissed. A similar rule has been adopted for the state and local courts in New York State. Also, defendants in jail for more than ninety days, if they are not charged with homicide, are to be released upon bond or their own recognizance pending trial, unless the prosecution can persuade a court that there are exceptional circumstances warranting the delay.

It is too soon to predict what the effect of these rules will be on the problem of delay. Massive additional resources are needed to permit implementation of the rules, and at this point we can only speculate whether they will be provided by the city, state, and/or federal governments. It would be tragic if they are withheld. An imponderable is how much latitude thec ourts will give prosecutors in explaining why cases have not been tried within the stipulated time periods.

PLEA BARGAINING

Perhaps the most obvious contradiction between what the court process really is and what it is supposed to be is the manner in which convictions are secured. The model is a trial in which all of the defendant's guaranteed rights are preserved and in which the evidence is carefully sifted by a jury of his peers. But trials simply cannot be provided in all cases. There are not nearly enough courtrooms, judges, prosecutors, defense lawyers or other court personnel to give trials to all but a few of those who are charged with crime.

Ninety percent of all convictions are secured by pleas of guilty. These pleas arise from negotiations between the prosecution and defense counsel, and sometimes the judge; and most of the plea "bargains" thus struck are accepted by the courts. Many times, particularly in less serious cases, plea negotiations take place during harried meetings in crowded corridors and even in courtrooms as the parties and their advocates are standing before the bench. Because of the pressing need to dispose of cases and the lack of sufficient time, prosecutors often agree to pleas without knowing much about the defendants, their backgrounds or their needs.

In almost every case resulting in a guilty plea the defendant has agreed to plead to one or more charges less serious than those leveled against him by the indictment or the information. This is the nub of the agreement. There would be little reason for the defendant to waive his right to be tried on the charges, even if his chances of acquittal were faint, if he did not receive something in return for his waiver. The negotiations usually revolve about the efforts of defense counsel to secure a plea less serious in degree than the crime charged and the prosecutor's attempt to obtain a plea which would most closely resemble the original charge.

Several factors influence the negotiations, one of the most important being the time available to the prosecution to deal with other cases awaiting trial. Thus, a defendant will profit by plea bargaining during a particularly busy time of the year for the prosecutor. The busier the prosecutor is, in fact, the better the deal is apt to be for the defendant. Another important factor in plea negotiations is the pretrial status of the defendant. If he is free pending trial he is in no particular rush to be sentenced. If, on the other hand, he is in detention—and, as we have observed, in large urban areas pretrial detention usually takes place in uncomfortable, overcrowded facilities—he is more anxious to wind up the prosecution, even if it means being sent to a correctional institution. Many defendants prefer to serve time in prisons or penitentiaries, where some facilities for recreation and work exist, as opposed to pretrial detention facilities known for overcrowding and idleness.

Detained defendants are especially motivated to plead guilty when the plea would have the effect of setting them free. People charged with petty offenses often face the likely prospect, if convicted, of receiving suspended sentences. If they are in pretrial detention, obviously they will be under pressure to plead guilty just to get out of jail. People charged with more serious offenses may also be able to secure their freedom if they plead guilty and receive sentences of "time [already] served" or sentences which approximate the time they have spent in jail on pretrial detention. This occurs with some frequency in areas where it takes one to two years to obtain trials.

Overcrowding in detention facilities has motivated court officials to rely more heavily than ever on plea negotiations. The 1970 riots in New York City's detention facilities demonstrated the need to dispose of cases more quickly in the courts. The mayor of the city of New York and the head of the Department of Correction as well as the prisoners urged the courts to move more quickly in order to shorten the stay of defendants awaiting trial or sentence. The courts responded as best they could, but since they were not given enormously strengthened resources their efforts were not very productive.

Defendants welcome plea bargaining in most instances to reduce the maximum sentences which may be levied against them. A typical indictment in a serious case cites three, four or five crimes which could bring an aggregate thirty-, forty-, or fifty-year jail sentence. In order to reduce the possible maximum sentence, the defendant negotiates for a plea to one or two of the crimes or to a crime reflecting an attempt to commit a criminal act—which carries a shorter sentence than for conviction on the consummated act—or to a "lesser included offense" not listed in the indictment. As long as prison sentences on individual crimes are placed at twenty to thirty years each, defendants will strive to limit the maximum sentences which could be imposed. A defendant charged, for example, with robbery and possession of a weapon who succeeds in obtaining a plea of guilty to an attempted larceny may have limited the power of the judge presiding to sentence him to two and a half years in prison instead of thirty or forty years.

Guilty pleas to reduced charges have been criticized for resulting in convictions for crimes other than those actually committed. Generally, the plea is to a lesser count which is related to the more serious crime originally charged. A defendant charged with robbery may be permitted to plead guilty to the less serious count of larceny or assault—which are elements of the original charge. Sometimes a count must be manufactured to permit the defendant to plead to a less serious crime. In a nationally televised documentary it was recently revealed that in Denver, Colorado, defendants arrested for burglary were permitted at times to plead guilty to the less serious crime of possession of burglar's tools even though they actually had no burglar's tools when they committed their crimes. Similarly, a carload of youths found with marijuana in a suburb of New York City were permitted to plead guilty to the less serious offense of public intoxication although they were not intoxicated at the time of their arrest.

Undoubtedly, there is some impairment of the credibility of the criminal-justice system when defendants plead guilty to offenses which they did not commit, in an effort to avoid being tried for crimes which they did. Furthermore, the conditions under which pleas of guilty are taken have periodically brought the courts under heavy criticism for obvious hypocrisy. Typically, after being promised a dismissal of the remaining charges in return for a plea to one of the charges (and possibly a promise of a specific sentence) the defendant is asked whether he was made any promises for his decision to plead guilty and he must dutifully reply "No." Everyone in the courtroom knows that there was an understanding reached as a result of the plea negotiations, but the law demands that this be denied in open court as proof that the plea was voluntary.

Many judges do not play an active role in plea negotiations, leaving the bargaining to the attorneys and then ruling on the agreed-upon plea. In large urban areas where obtaining dispositions and reducing backlogs are a major and sometimes overriding concern, some judges feel obligated to take a more active role in the negotiations. They may in some instances suggest to defendants the sentences which would be imposed in return for pleas of guilty. The judge who "bargains" impairs his role as an impartial arbiter and diminishes the stature of the judicial process in the eyes of all participants. Consider, for example, the serious problem presented when a defendant declines an offer made or approved by a judge. It is doubtful whether that defendant can go to trial with a feeling that the judge is impartial. Besides the subjective factor—the apprehension that a judge may be peeved at having his offer declined—there is the problem of all the background history, including a defendant's prior criminal record, which has already come to the judge's attention. It is generally recommended, quite soundly, that in such a case the judge should disqualify himself from conducting the proceedings even though the case is to be tried before a jury.

The defendant who pleads guilty to a lesser crime is given a special reward for saving the time and expense of a trial—a sharp reduction in the ceiling of sentence. Some judges rationalize this leniency by suggesting that the plea is the first step toward rehabilitation—purportedly constituting a recognition by the defendant that he has committed a wrong against society. This is sheer nonsense in view of the fact that the dominant theme of all the promises and pressures placed upon the defendant to plead is to minimize the dimensions of that wrong.

Because plea bargaining is conducted in secret it is not always possible to determine the precise scope of the agreement. It is obvious at times when a person pleads guilty to a reduced charge and the prosecutor moves to dismiss the higher charge that both are elements of the plea negotiations. The question of sentencing sometimes enters the negotiations. The prosecutor may promise to recommend a lenient sentence, and sometimes the judge will offer a hint as to the nature of the sentence. These references to the sentence often lead to a series of nasty charges and countercharges. Prisoners regularly claim they were misled or deceived; in many thousands of proceedings brought in court each year (by what are called "writs of error coram nobis") they argue that their pleas were exacted by unfulfilled promises or that they were pressured to plead guilty by the threat of heavy sentences. Since the negotiations are not recorded there is no way of determining who is right (or who is more right than wrong). One solution to this problem as well as to the problem of the precarious role of the presiding judge would be to record the full extent of the negotiations in advance of the plea. Thus the terms of the agreement, including a statement concerning what was said, if anything, about the sentence, would be spelled out for the record. The judge, under one proposed plan, would not engage in the plea negotiations; he would merely state his agreement or disagreement with the result of the negotiations between the prosecution and defense. In this way the higher courts would be in a far better position to determine whether there was any undue influence in obtaining the plea.

The chances of eliminating plea bargaining are extremely slim. As long as legislatures continue to attach excessive prison sentences to criminal conduct, defendants will seek and indeed feel enormous pressure to minimize the length of the prison sentence they will be given if convicted. And as long as there are not enough courtrooms, public defenders, prosecutors, judges, and nonjudicial court personnel to try all cases promptly, pleas will be sought by prosecutors.

There is nothing sacrosanct about plea negotiations or pleas of guilty. It is only out of necessity that they persist to such an extent. In theory, plea bargaining and guilty pleas can be eliminated. Every case could go to trial. The defendant may acknowledge guilt if he sees fit, and the prosecution may present whatever evidence is not embraced by the plea. The judge presiding would then have all of the facts before him and would be in a better position to render an intelligent judgment.

Even in a fully resourced and most efficient court system, a fair measure of plea discussions—as opposed to plea bargaining, with all its invidious aspects—would be highly desirable. First, a full and fair exchange between prosecutor and defense counsel could disclose the strengths and weaknesses of their cases and in some instances lead to dismissal either of the charges or of individual counts in the indictment which cannot be proven; or, conversely, it could persuade a defendant that he stands little chance of winning an acquittal.

In many cases, particularly those involving first and youthful offenders, it is shortsighted and unwise to expose defendants to conviction to the full extent of the serious crimes with which they may technically and legally be charged. For example, in the case of a quartet of high-school boys who dared each other into taking a neighbor's car for a joy ride and who were correctly, under the law, indicted for the felony of grand larceny, should the defendants be forced to trial and subjected to the danger of being branded as felons for the rest of their lives? Or should they be permitted to plead to the misdemeanor of petit larceny or even an offense such as disorderly conduct? As a practical matter, juries are loath to convict when the punishment can far exceed the community's notion of what befits the gravity of the offense.

Hard and fast conclusions about plea bargaining are difficult to draw. With less than perfect conditions in the courts, it provides benefit to defendants and to the system. The media and the public should make greater efforts to understand the need for a reformed plea-bargaining process and what it would take, in terms of massive financial assistance, to achieve one.

MANAGEMENT OF THE COURTS

The business of the courts is to move large numbers of cases through a series of stages while meeting certain strict standards of fairness. A variety of personnel engage in these tasks. Just as in any large business, the successful operation of the undertaking depends on proper utilization of personnel and resources, intelligent short- and long-range planning, and an administrative structure designed to achieve optimum efficiency. A business heavily engaged in clerical work should take reasonable steps to ensure that its record forms and clerical procedures are efficient, that its employees are not bogged down in unnecessary chores, and that appropriate office and data-processing equipment is being used. The operation of the courts is characterized by poor utilization of manpower and resources and the employment of clerical and administrative practices which were abandoned by business decades ago.

Courts are in desperate need of streamlined record-keeping and filing procedures and of modern data-processing approaches and equipment. Important as it is to have more judges, clerks, court reporters and secretaries, sound clerical and management techniques in the courts are essential and should be a top priority of court administrators as well as local, state and federal government. Business management techniques, too long absent from the courts, would be particularly helpful in a system where clerical and administrative procedures are cumbersome, antiquated and inefficient. Court record forms and record-keeping devices are crude, require repetitive entries, and cause wasted effort and delays. Record keeping in the courts today often fails to use such basic clerical tools as multiple-ply forms; the same information is often recorded by several agencies at various stages of proceedings. A serious problem confronting judges is the difficulty of deciphering notations on official court papers. Handwritten entries are so difficult to read that the judge presiding often is unable to interpret entries made at earlier stages. Moreover, the forms used are not standardized and often vary within the same jurisdiction.

There are many other symptoms of the lack of modern management concepts in the courts. Hundreds of people are expected to report to the same courtroom at the same time, although many are certain to wait for hours for their cases to be called. Adjournments are granted for reasons which, if made known earlier, could have avoided wasted appearances for lawyers, police officers, defendants and witnesses. High-salaried clerks are assigned menial tasks. Too much clerical time is spent making the same handwritten entries in hardbound ledger books and then again in other records. Notices to lawyers, defendants, police officers and other witnesses often are written by hand or typed slowly by court clerks (earning, in some instances, twelve to fifteen thousand dollars a year). Often, the few statistics which are gathered are filed and never used; other statistics which could be of assistance (in underscoring problems of court backlogs and delays in processing of cases) are not kept.

Financial assistance is needed for analyses of court management, for revision of outdated and unproductive records and record-keeping devices, and for the application of modern technological advances. Management and data-processing consultants must be employed to revise procedures and to create better administrative control and coordination. Every court system must be given the financial resources to hire a professional administrator supported by a capable staff. Systems analysts and statisticians must become part of the administrative staff; they can be hired only if salaries are sufficiently attractive to compete with private industry.

While relatively little progress has been made in meeting these conditions in the courts over the past few decades, private industry has employed technical management expertise, mastered new systems approaches, and generally improved clerical operations. Several industries have used computers to gather data, store it and then provide it almost immediately upon request in a variety of useful forms. One illustration of the use of terminals to provide data is the small televisionlike screen that securities brokers use. Stock quotations are obtained on the screen within seconds of requesting the information by pressing one or two buttons below the screen. One automated quotations system gives bid and asked prices on some 2,500 counter stocks. As stock prices change they are fed into the computer, which spews out the data upon request.

Making data available in appropriate forms and at appropriate times is one of the greatest contributions that computers can make to the court system. At several key points within the criminal-justice system there is a pressing need for information, which may not have been gathered or which may be in the bottom of a file cabinet and not brought to the attention of the presiding judge, the prosecutor or defense counsel. It is not uncommon, in fact, for one or more agencies to have relevant information which is not routinely shared with other agencies with similar responsibilities or with the court. One of the earliest information needs in the court process concerns the question of bail, which, as we have seen, is based on a prediction as to whether the defendant will return to court. His roots in the community—his employment record, family ties, and length of time in the jurisdiction—as well as any prior criminal record which may exist are important data needed by the magistrate. Even today the information presented to the court sometimes does not even include, because of the abominable state of court records, a clear picture of the defendant's history of returning to court on prior occasions. Similarly, the sentencing decision is often based on nothing more than the defendant's prior criminal record. And as one reflection of the real crisis facing the courts, it is not uncommon, in some areas at least, for such criminal histories to be incomplete and inaccurate.

The important role that computers can play in the courts is not limited to providing data upon request. A large number of notices and other formal legal documents must be distributed daily to witnesses, attorneys, correctional officials, bail bondsmen and others. Computers are especially equipped to perform this function. They can also provide valuable statistical reports to administrators in a variety of forms which would not be practical to produce by manual procedures. Vast amounts of clerical time could be saved by these modern methods and machinery in many large urban areas, and the results would be more accurate.

The potential of computers in the courts as a valuable management tool has not been tapped. They have been used in the courts for isolated clerical tasks and for the handling of traffic infraction cases. Often the only computer in a citywide court system is in Traffic Court. As might be expected, the use of computers has proved a valuable asset in processing traffic infraction cases and in collecting fines. The Chicago collection delays decreased from eight months to one month after a computer was installed to monitor traffic tickets. Computers in St. Louis and Washington, D.C., in addition to matching traffic tickets for the names and addresses of automobile owners, print Traffic Court calendars, notices of intent to issue a warrant, arrest warrants, and notices of judgment. In San

Diego, a master citation file is placed in computer storage and before accepting fines a clerk can press a button and discover whether prior citations are outstanding. This kind of application would serve a variety of valuable uses in a criminal-court process hungry for information and inundated by record-keeping and record-producing requirements.

The most advanced application of modern data-processing techniques in the courts is in the Philadelphia Common Pleas Court, where a computer is used as a management tool to produce a large variety of court statistics and documents—court calendars, subpoenas, notices to appear in court, and lists of eligible jurors, prisoners to be delivered to court each day, grand-jury indictments, dispositions of cases, available courtrooms, and bench warrants. The computer-generated statistics provide immeasurable assistance to administrators in planning for short- and long-range needs and in identifying problems which require attention. The Philadelphia computer, continually fed with current information, also handles the complex and very troublesome task of scheduling cases, with due consideration given to certain important priorities (older cases, serious cases, multi-witness cases) and to the availability of attorneys, witnesses and courtrooms. Visual display units, resembling television screens, have been placed in some Philadelphia courtrooms, and within seconds the judges presiding can retrieve important information about defendants appearing before them.

The computer in Philadelphia has been credited with reducing backlogs and permitting faster disposition of cases. Unquestionably it is not a complete answer to a heavy volume of cases and cannot substitute for shortages in personnel, but its value as a tool in the handling of large numbers of cases and in the proper administration of the courts is incalculable.

An assessment of court operations reveals the need for strengthened management. In some areas there are literally hundreds of autonomous courts concerned with their own budgetary and personnel problems. Rules of court, allocations of manpower, and calendaring techniques sometimes are made within each of many courts in a jurisdiction, and each operates independently of the others. In these jurisdictions one court is filled to capacity while another nearby finishes its business by noon; no provision is made for balancing the workloads. In other jurisdictions there is centralized administration—a unified court system—with control over the operation of all courts generally placed in the state's highest court.

Proper planning for court needs, uniformity in rules governing court procedures, and intelligent allocation of manpower can best be accomplished where there is centralized administration. To illustrate how central authority may be exerted to meet a crisis: each of the four appellate divisions in New York State has authority to make intercourt transfers of judicial personnel and to use court facilities in its jurisdiction as it sees fit. This permits the use of civil-court personnel and facilities for the processing of criminal cases whenever backlogs reach critical proportions. In January 1968, as Presiding Justice of the Appellate Division, First Department, I noted an inordinately large and growing backlog of criminal cases in Bronx County. I directed that all but one of the trial parts in the civil branch of the Supreme Court in Bronx County, the court of general jurisdiction for the trial of both civil and criminal cases, be closed down for one month to handle the increasing number of criminal indictments. Enormous inroads were made, and, for a short period at least, the criminal calendars became manageable. Similar deployment of resources is made as a regular course in administering the courts in New York City—precisely because there is centralized administration of the courts.

Centralized administration will have little impact in the absence of strengthened authority and the tools to carry out management responsibilities. Professional administrative and technical assistance must be provided. Presiding or chief judges must have capable staffs with a variety of management skills. Their hands must be strengthened by laws giving them strong supervisory power over all judicial and nonjudicial court personnel.

SENTENCING

The sentencing stage represents the bridge between the guilt-determining process (in the courts) and the rehabilitative or punitive process (in corrections). Too often sentence is rendered by a judge with insufficient information about the offender and insufficient assistance in developing appropriate rehabilitative programs. To add to these inadequacies, we know too little about how to rehabilitate offenders to make intelligent judgments at sentencing time.

Since pre-sentencing reports are customary only in felony cases, in most instances the sole bases upon which sentencing decisions are made are limited background data about defendants and the crimes, if any, that they have committed. The alternative in sentencing is, fundamentally, probation or prison. Probation is release to the community, subject to checking in with a probation officer periodically, either in person or by mail; prison is total restriction, surrender of all the familiar forms of freedom and living by arbitrary rules in an environment totally unlike the one in society. Sentencing discretion is naturally limited by the nature of the crime to which the defendant has pleaded.

James V. Bennett, former director of the Federal Bureau of Prisons, claims that sentences in this country are "the most severe in the world." [15] His view is supported by the report of the National Crime Commission, which observed that most people sent to prison do not belong there. Sentencing practices vary widely from jurisdiction to jurisdiction and from case to case. Bennett contends that in no other nation are "extreme and widespread inequities" so prevalent. Instances of long-term imprisonment and sentence disparity have been recorded over the years. Bennett cites these disparities, among others, from the experiences in the federal courts: an eighteen-year prison term to a novice check forger in one court, and a six-month sentence to an experienced check forger in a nearby court; a fifteen-year prison term to a check forger with no prior criminal record, and a thirty-day jail term to another forger who had two prior convictions ("simply because they appeared before two different judges").

The steady increase in narcotics prosecutions in all sections of the country has given rise to a wide and disparate range of sentences to offenders. In the large cities, where narcotics problems are more numerous, sentences are far less severe than elsewhere. Possession-of-narcotics crimes often are treated as minor offenses which upon conviction result in suspended sentences. Even narcotics sellers in large cities have been permitted to plead to misdemeanors and have served no more than five- or six-month jail sentences. But in other areas of the country marijuana possession has brought ten- to twenty-year prison terms and the sale of narcotics and dangerous drugs has been treated as a major crime.

A five-year Congressional study of federal-court sentencing practices cited by Bennett revealed major differences among jurisdictions.

Sentences for stealing an automobile, according to this study, averaged twelve months in New Hampshire, whereas in northern Oklahoma the average was 43.8 months. Average prison terms in general varied from 11.7 months in northern New York to fifty-two months in Iowa. Studies of sentencing practices in state courts reveal similar differences. The median time served by all felons sentenced to prison in Vermont was eight months, according to one study, and in Illinois thirty-one months.

Recently, during the course of some state and federally sponsored conferences for judges, hypothetical cases were presented to participant jurists, who were asked to state the type of sentence they would impose. They were supplied with probation reports and other data comparable to the information they would rely on when actually performing their sentencing functions. Widespread variations by the conferees were common. The results of one reported conference, for example, revealed that, of fifty-four judges, twenty-six said they would impose a fine or place the defendant on probation, while twenty-eight others said they would imprison the defendant for one year or more. In another instance, the variation of votes by participating judges on the same set of facts extended from probation to a twenty-year term of imprisonment.[16]

It need hardly be said that sentence disparity and severity engender indelible bitterness and hostility among those defendants who believe they have been treated unfairly. Any attempt to reform the system should place considerable priority on minimizing dissimilarities in sentencing and perhaps reducing the length of most prison terms. An American Bar Association study group, finding that there were "far too many long-term commitments" and that sentences in excess of five years are rare in most European countries, recently urged five-year maximum sentences for most felonies,[17] but no significant effort to adopt this recommendation has been made to date. Other legislative reforms should include the repeal of "mandatory minimum" legislation which in some jurisdictions removes discretion from the court in placing offenders on probation and issuing light sentences. There is simply no justification for mandating a minimum sentence for all people convicted of certain crimes. Individual backgrounds and the facts of each case, as well as the individual rehabilitative needs of defendants, should always be the basis for sentencing decisions.

One of the most provocative ideas suggested to improve sentencing practices is the transfer of the sentencing responsibility to a tribunal of behavioral scientists. Such a proposal was made several decades ago by Sheldon Glueck, who sought the establishment of "socio-penal commissions" composed of lawyers, psychiatrists, psychologists and sociologists, who would presumably be better qualified to determine and prescribe individualized treatment for convicted offenders. The closest we have come to implementing the tribunal concept is in the state of Washington, where the court sets the maximum sentence. A Board of Prison Terms and Parole, after reviewing the prisoner's background and development in prison, sets the minimum sentence to be served. After one year has been served the Board may reconsider and modify the sentence. Other states, relying primarily on the court to set jail terms, give parole boards considerable discretion to release prisoners before the full term is served. The boards are empowered to release prisoners after they have served fractions such as one fourth, one third, or one half of the sentence. In other cases, notably with sexual offenders, parole authorities are usually given more explicit discretion in determining the length of sentences. A sentence of "one day to life," for example, provides enormous, life-span discretion in the hands of a parole board to determine how long a prisoner is to be deprived of his liberty.

The debate over whether sentencing authority should be retained by the court centers on the question of who is best qualified to determine the most appropriate sentences. Reliance on behavioral scientists is understandable; certainly there are other professions which know a great deal more than judges do about human behavior. But we must guard against the very tempting notion that those who have studied human behavior have a monopoly of information in this area or a thorough enough understanding to predict behavioral patterns in individual cases.

Extreme caution should be taken against removing this entire function from the courts. We must do more to make judges aware of the futility and unfairness of lengthy jail terms generally, and do much more to give to judges the information needed to make rational sentencing judgments. Sentencing tribunals, with members drawn from several relevant disciplines, should perhaps be established, as urged by Glueck, to make recommendations to the courts on the length of sentences. But the final decision, in my opinion, should be left in the hands of the sentencing judge who is detached from the disciplines and trained to sift expert opinions; and most convicted offenders probably would be of the same view.

One of the great dilemmas faced by the courts is that there are so few meaningful sentencing alternatives: release to the community

—either with no supervision or with the minimal supervision provided by overworked probation officials—or imprisonment. Either alternative is too rigid and offers too little tolerance for the special and individual needs of most defendants.

IX CORRECTIONS

CORRECTIONAL TREATMENT WITHIN PENAL INSTITUTIONS

A shocking shortcoming of penal institutions is that so little is done to prepare inmates for life outside the institution. A national study of penal institutions conducted in 1966 by the National Council on Crime and Delinquency revealed that prisoners receive little guidance and almost no occupational training that would equip them to hold steady jobs in society.[1] The study showed that in sixty-five percent of the nation's short-term institutions, where sentences of one year or less are served, there was not a single rehabilitation program of any sort, and the few work programs were poorly organized, poorly equipped and poorly supervised.

The emphasis within prisons (short-term and long-term) is on security and on holding prisoners until they serve their required time. Few trained teachers, social workers and psychologists serve on staffs of penal institutions. Where a psychologist is available he is responsible for assisting, on the average, more than four thousand inmates. The limited available funds are used to hire more prison guards, and, unfortunately, the low salaries offered do not always attract the most sympathetic or committed persons. The median salary range for a prison guard in 1966 was found to be four to five thousand dollars a year, and in more than half the states there was no minimum educational requirement for this position. Even more distressing is the fact that in about half the states there was no minimum educational requirement for the institution's top position of superintendent. The median salary range for this position in 1966 was seven to eight thousand a year.

One authoritative source cites the rigid and simplistic attitudes of correctional workers as a major problem in creating reform within penal institutions.[2] He maintains that the concept of inmates as dangerous people requiring constant surveillance and control limits the ability or desire of the staff to work constructively with incarcerated offenders. Even the professional staff, according to this commentator, displays rigidities in its approach to offenders which obstruct needed changes in penal programs.

The lack of meaningful training programs in penal institutions is, in itself, an indictment of our entire criminal-justice system. The high proportion of parole violations and subsequent returns to prison is plain evidence of the failure of institutionalization. We simply have not looked upon prison terms as our opportunity to deal with people who, for some reason or combination of reasons, have a tendency to commit serious crimes. When so many who are held for several years return to lives of crime it should be the clearest indication that we have failed in our obligation to them and to ourselves. This failure should force us to examine what we have done and what we have failed to do when they were confined.

A twelve-year Virginia study demonstrated a clear relationship between low earnings and a high ratio of parole violations; more than forty percent of those released on parole who had monthly incomes of less than fifty dollars violated parole, while only ten percent of those earning more than $275 per month did so.[3] Although this study does not offer ironclad proof that low earnings are causally related to crime, it should be sufficient to encourage the introduction into penal institutions of vocational guidance and training programs to train prisoners to become skilled workers. Some vocational training exists, but much more has to be done in this area. Opposition by labor unions and private industry to outside distribution of prison-produced goods has stunted realistic work programs and job training within the institutions. For the most part prison labor has been relegated to producing goods for tax-supported and nonprofit purposes.

The President's Commission on Crime in the District of Columbia reported recently on vocational training in the District of Columbia Reformatory for Men, an institution which houses male prisoners serving sentences of more than one year: "It maintains 11 industrial operations, including a pattern shop, foundry, print shop, furniture repair shop, broom, brush and mattress shop, machine shop, and tag and sign shop." [4] The Commission justifiably concluded: "Unfortunately, much of the vocational training equips inmates to do a job within the institution only, and in many cases bears little relation to work opportunities available in the community." This observation concerns a reformatory, an institution supposedly dedicated to the reformation of those who have committed crimes. Much less can be said for institutions which house prisoners for shorter terms and those which are located in poorer jurisdictions unable to afford vocational training and related programs, as well as those not specifically charged with reforming prisoners. Summing up this failure, one former prisoner asked, "Did you ever try looking for a job making license plates?" [5]

Rehabilitation within these institutions is also impeded by poor designing of the physical plant, ill-equipped facilities, and inadequate ventilation, heating, light and space. Prison life is unpleasant, cruelly monotonous, dehumanizing and sometimes brutal. Prisoners live in tiny cubicles, several sometimes sharing space built to accommodate one prisoner. A series of prison riots has recently focused attention on a variety of inhumane conditions under which prisoners are compelled to live, whether awaiting trial or serving sentences. Ranging from the inferior quality of food to severe physical brutality, these conditions harden existing antisocial attitudes. Solitary confinement is still widespread, and only recently have the courts begun to review prisoners' applications challenging these and other forms of punishment.

Arbitrary decision-making appears to be widespread, perhaps a direct result of a history of a hands-off policy by the courts. Punishment is imposed in the absence of any of the procedural safeguards present during the pre-correction stage of the system when suspects are processed by the police and the courts. Loss of privileges, including visitation, recreation, mail and early release, are imposed summarily. And apart from the question of punishment, the privileges themselves are unduly limited. Many institutions allow visiting only once a month. Restrictions upon incoming and outgoing mail are widespread. Even the frequency with which letters may be sent is regulated; all mail is censored in some institutions, although in others letters to attorneys and to certain public officials may be sent uncensored. Some prison rules provide that "false" statements made by prisoners may be censored and may be the basis for punishment. In some institutions there is a rule against including any "controversial" discussion in outgoing mail, and many institutions prohibit criticism of the law, institutional policies, and officials.

Rigid, often arbitrary rules control all aspects of prison life.[6] These rules for the most part are not designed to teach inmates how to adjust to living in the community which they will ultimately reenter, but are intended to maintain strict discipline within the penal institution. Even certain common forms of language are prohibited. One commentator observes that references to solitary confinement by the commonly used term "the hole" would subject prisoners in some institutions to punishment.[7] Describing a prison official as a "creep" in a personal diary that also contained statements manifesting sexual desires toward two female staff members resulted recently in twenty days in solitary confinement and other punishment for a prisoner held in a New York State institution.[8] The National Crime Commission observed that "extremes of deprivation, strict discipline, and punishment . . . make institutions impersonal, quasi-military places." [9]

The chief psychiatrist of a California correctional facility, acknowledging the inhumanity of prison life, views the imposition of strict controls over prisoners as a poor way of making people change.[10] He says that such primitive measures merely generate "more and more rage and hostility." He adds that they lead to the very behavior which they are meant to suppress. Since these measures give rise to smoldering resentment, society suffers at the hands of prisoners after their release from prison.

The very nature of prison life, in addition to the hostility engendered by the punitive atmosphere, causes brutality among the prisoners. Sexual starvation breeds large-scale homosexuality, much of it forced upon weaker and younger prisoners. A show of force—by acts of violence on other prisoners—is felt necessary by prisoners to stave off homosexual attacks and to be part of what one prisoner refers to as the "hierarchy" of a caste system. He says, "Sometimes it would be necessary to punch a guy in the mouth for crossing a certain line or looking at you for too long." [11]

The extent to which violence and other crime have taken hold of some of the prisons in this country was portrayed recently by a publicized decision of a West Virginia judge that incarceration of a young holdup man in the Moundsville, West Virginia, penitentiary constituted cruel and unusual punishment in violation of the United States Constitution. The petitioner had testified that he had been sexually attacked by two men within eyesight of a correctional officer.[12] One year earlier a prisoner had petitioned the judge in fear of his life. Two days before the scheduled court hearing the prisoner was murdered. According to the local prosecutor the murder resulted from rival gang warfare for control of the prison. "He was killed," said the prosecutor, "merely as an object lesson to the other inmates that, in effect, 'when we say jump, you jump.' " Since that time another prisoner has been murdered—the sixth in five years—over the homosexual favors of a fellow prisoner. The warden of Moundsville penitentiary stated recently that there was "no way on earth" he could guarantee the safety of any inmate in the institution.

In the recent case in which the court rules that it would be cruel and unusual punishment to send a defendant to Moundsville, the prosecutor testified: "I won't now as a policy of my office ask the court to sentence a man to the penitentiary unless I consider him a complete loss, an irrevocable loss to society . . . a throwaway . . . and if he goes to the penitentiary . . . what we are doing to that man is, in my opinion, infinitely worse than anything he could ever have done to society."

Penal institutions for detention and short-term as well as long-term sentences must be changed structurally and operationally for those who must be incarcerated. They should be smaller and less restrictive. Maximum-security fortresses have been proven unnecessary for most prisoners. More and better programs in long-term and short-term penal institutions must be expanded for work experience and vocational training for skilled jobs, and living conditions within the institutions must be substantially improved. Prisoners should be treated with greater dignity and permitted to live under reasonable rules and regulations, with much less emphasis on mass handling and regimentation. Those who are able to maintain family relationships should be encouraged to do so; periodic weekend furloughs for selected prisoners should be permitted. This is precisely the kind of correctional program being used in Sweden, where the focus seems to be on the prisoner's eventual reentry into society.

It is a paradox that the United States, which places a premium, in the very fabric of its government, on the rights of its citizens, has so much to learn from some other countries about the treatment of prisoners.[13] Mail censorship is a thing of the past in Sweden. For many years married prisoners in Mexico have been permitted conjugal visitation with their spouses, whereas in only one institution in Mississippi and, more recently, in California has that been permitted in this country. Various programs allowing prisoners to leave penal institutions for periods of time have been used in Belgium, Latin America and the Scandinavian countries. In Sweden prisoners get home leave every three or four months, a program in existence since 1937. Almost all prisoners in Sweden, in fact, get periodic two- to three-day "furloughs" from their places of incarceration. Wives are permitted, even in the largest of Sweden's prisons, to visit their husbands in the privacy of locked rooms. There are family prisons in Sweden in which even murderers live with their families and work in the community during the day. Explaining what one correctional authority has called the "relatively peaceful atmosphere" of Sweden's largest prison (population two hundred), a Swedish inmate provided this insight:

> . . . we are treated fairly, and we really have a sort of freedom and responsibility. In this way there aren't any specific groups which try to be in command of the other guys . . . That is why you in America have prison riots. Because the harder they treat us, the harder we will be, and the fairer they treat us, the fairer we will be.[14]

The prison system in Finland since 1947 has undergone many progressive reforms, including the formation of sensible training programs and modernization of institutions. Wages paid prisoners are comparable to those received in civil service. The use of labor colonies, with no locked doors or windows, is widespread: more than forty percent of all imprisoned persons serve their sentences working in "open institutions." These institutions permit an easier adjustment to the community where prisoners eventually return. The system is also used widely in Sweden, and in Japan prisoners work side by side with nonprison workers in the shipbuilding industry. In Sweden there are eighty-eight prisons for approximately five thousand prisoners, with an average of one staff person for every two prisoners. Idleness is rare and inmates receive wages for their work in a factory or agricultural setting. And even in the larger Swedish institutions the physical plant is consistent with rehabilitation goals. Dormitories, colorful décor, recreational facilities, and well-lit rooms are typical.

Another knowledgeable commentator who viewed Swedish prisons at first hand concludes that in Sweden a "humanitarian and egalitarian attitude is indeed the mainspring of the whole correctional system." He says that the Swedish prisoner "still remains a Swedish citizen meriting respect, continuing properly to enjoy a quite high standard of living, and remaining a part of the community." [15] The guards are polite, and a Swedish ombudsman charged with investigating civilian complaints against abuses by government officials takes prisoners' complaints quite seriously.

Paradoxically, in this country there is substantial documentation of the cruelty of prison life, but too little understanding and concern by the public at large. It does not require an ombudsman to document the fact that prison life in the United States is extraordinarily cruel. There is a great need to call attention to the dehumanizing conditions and to remind people that prisoners are persons who have, or should have, certain rights and who will eventually take their places in society. Drastic action is needed to change the form of prisons, to make them habitable and responsive to individual needs. Smaller prisons, more comfortable living quarters, frequent furloughs, relevant job training and work experience, counseling, and a marked movement away from regimentation, arbitrary rules and punishment would constitute a program for change.

The reintegration of prisoners into society should be a major goal of corrections. One of the most innovative attempts in the prisons to accomplish this goal is "work release," a program in which certain inmates are permitted during the latter stages of their incarceration to work at jobs in the community during the day and to return at night to the institution. By the time they are released on parole, the inmates have jobs which they have held for several months and they have gained some measure of acceptance in the outside world and some sense of comfort in it. They are also given the opportunity of becoming acclimated to a comparatively permissive community which in many respects differs radically from the rigid and regimented one in prison. While work-release programs are no guarantee that the released inmates will be model citizens, the risk of their continuing their past deviant practices is reduced, particularly if they are able to earn adequate salaries.

Unfortunately, the move to establish work-release programs, being highly controversial, has been making slow progress, and the result is that we have been remiss in using this technique to bridge the gap between life within the institution and life in the community. For the most part the few programs begun have been limited to misdemeanants. A few states permit felons to take part in work release, but not all have implemented the program. Unlike most other areas, in Delaware twenty-three percent of prisoners are enrolled in such a program. Virginia has an education-release program in which prisoners attend educational institutions outside the prison. Experience has shown that relatively few prisoners—three percent in one institution, eight in another—have used the release programs to attempt escapes.[16]

Neither our laws nor our attitudes indicate any concern for the ex-convict's reentry into society. In the movies of thirty years ago, Humphrey Bogart received a new suit and a ten-dollar bill as he said goodbye to the warden. Times have not changed. It is doubtful whether wardens still have time to extend their best wishes, and a ten-dollar bill does not purchase much any more. Universities have placement offices to obtain jobs for their graduates; prisons do not. An "ex-con" is apt to lose a job, in fact, if his former status is discovered.

The statute law itself is a barrier to the rehabilitation of former prisoners. Instead of prohibiting discrimination in employment for these people, it prohibits them from holding certain jobs. Typically, in many communities a former convict with a felony conviction cannot obtain a license to practice the profession of real-estate broker, salesman, podiatrist, accountant, undertaker, embalmer, insurance adjuster, or private investigator. He will surely be fired if he works in a billiard parlor or in a restaurant where alcohol is sold—his employer is risking his license by having a felon on the payroll. We do not even allow a felon to vote.

Melvin Rivers, president of the Fortune Society and a former prisoner, provided this graphic account of the difficulties faced by an ex-con who chooses to lead a constructive life:

WHEN THE EX-OFFENDER COMES HOME . . .*

When I got out of prison in 1962, I had intentions of getting a barber's license, because I'd been the institutional barber in the prison and had a slip of paper that certified I'd spent 2,400 hours barbering. But when I applied at a barber shop, I had to start as a shine boy, even though I told the boss how much hair I'd cut, and showed him what I could do. He said he couldn't put me on a chair until I got a license. But the license never came. I got a note back saying the City couldn't give me one because of my record. The boss said to reapply, and I did, but the same thing happened again.

Later I worked in a real estate shop, but I couldn't get a salesman's license. A little later I found out that the guy working with me was also an ex-con, but he was using another man's broker's license and later got into a complicated mess. He told me he was submitting my application for a license, and I could work as a salesman while we waited for it to come. So I did, and was renting apartments for about five months until I got wise and asked him what was going on. Eventually I found the application in his drawer—he hadn't even sent it in. He said, "I'll tell you the truth, man, you can't get a license. I didn't want to tell you because I didn't want to hurt you, and I liked your potential." That's when I found out he was an ex-con, too.

I stayed on there a while anyway and made a little money, but then I cut out. I was going to go to nursing school, my Parole Officer

* Reprinted from *Fortune News,* November 1969; reprinted by permission of the author and The Fortune Society.

thought I'd be good at it. (He was the one Parole Officer who really helped me in seven years of parole.) He sent me to a nursing school. I asked about the course, and of course I had to tell them about my record. They said they were sorry, but they wouldn't be able to accept me.

Then I went across the street and applied for a security job at Kings County Hospital, and again I told the truth on the application. The guy came out and said he was sorry, but it was against City policy to hire me.

Then I worked at Downstate Medical Center for a while, and this time I didn't tell them anything. I got a job in their supply place, where I had to be bonded. But they ran a check on me, and I got fired.

Then I worked a year as an usher in a movie theatre, and they had an opening for manager in the same theatre, so I applied for it and the bonding sheet went out again, and I got fired, even though I'd worked there a year, and they liked me.

There was a construction job too, but the man said I couldn't get into the union because of the record, so I worked "off the books" and got paid in cash. But when my Parole Officer found out about it, he made me quit.

I worked in a laundry too for a while, but some baby clothes got stolen and when the manager asked me if I had a record and I said yes, he fired me, even though I told him I wasn't married and couldn't have any use for the stuff.

Then I worked in a car place, and one day I turned a car on that had been left in gear, and it crashed into another car. But they didn't fire me for that—they fired me because a bonding company said I had a record and I guess they figured I might steal a car, even though nothing was on my record about ever stealing a car.

I had a lot of trouble getting a driver's license, but after three years I finally got one. I applied for a bus driver's job, and I got very good scores on all the tests. But the City of New York informed me it was exercising its rights to choose only one out of every three people who applied.

I had a job driving a gypsy cab for a while, and it's a funny thing, I thought it was a parole violation to drive one of those cabs, because we all stopped to pick up people even though we weren't supposed to. So I never told my Parole Officer until I applied to get off parole. He said it wasn't a violation to drive a gypsy cab, but it was a violation not to have told him about it. So I had to serve two more years of parole.

One thing I'd always wanted to be was a singer, and I did cut a record. I even sang with a group for a while, but they had to let me go because I couldn't get a cabaret license to sing anywhere they sold alcoholic beverages.

Eventually I gave up, and went back into crime. I'd spent about three years trying to go straight, and it just seemed it wasn't going to work. And in prison I'd learned how to graduate from snatching pocketbooks and mugging to armed robbery, living off women, selling stolen goods, and dealing in reefers and cocaine. So I started a second criminal career.[17]

COMMUNITY-BASED CORRECTIONS

Parole, the early release of prisoners from penal institutions, appears not to have succeeded in integrating the offender into the community, primarily because the inadequately supported parole process is presently designed to do little more than maintain periodic communication between parole officers and parolees. Inmates are released from institutions and expected to reject past deviant behavioral patterns, although they are returned untrained and unprepared to the same environments which helped spawn their earlier criminal acts. Often they are placed under unreasonable restrictions concerning their personal lives and they view their parole officers as investigators trying to catch them in some technical violation of the conditions of their early release from prison.

The National Crime Commission suggested that institutionalization should be limited to a small percentage of convicted offenders. It urged that greater reliance be placed on community-based corrections—a strengthened probation service able to offer individualized care and supervision in a community setting.

Clearly, the most rational alternative to prison, one that is the most humane and the best suited to rehabilitation, is community treatment. The potential achievements of probation and parole are based upon the concept that individualized care in a community setting, with appropriate job or social counseling, can interrupt the crime cycle in individual cases. Reliance upon these correctional components, however, contemplates that those charged with the responsibility of offering the services have services to offer and the time to offer them properly. Both of these requisites to the adequate delivery of services do not exist in actual practice.

Probation and parole agencies lack both the manpower to deal satisfactorily with their large caseloads and the trained personnel to perform the necessary services. A recent national survey showed that ninety-seven percent of probationers under care are being supervised by probation officers who have caseloads comprising more than the recommended fifty cases each.[18] More than sixty-seven percent of probationers form part of caseloads greater than double the fifty-caseload standard.

For the most part, adequate community programs for people on probation do not exist. Employment training, in particular, is lacking, and in the absence of more knowledge about causes of crime it is safe to assume that the inability to command respectably paying jobs is probably a contributing factor to a continuing life of crime. In a recent national survey by the National Council on Crime and Delinquency, only twenty-seven percent of the probation agencies in the sample were found to offer imaginative programs for adult probationers.

It has been observed that although two thirds of the people within the correctional complex are on either probation or parole, only a small percentage of the total funds spent on corrections is devoted to community care.[19] Eighty percent of the corrections funds are spent on maintaining prisons. And most of that money is aimed at keeping prisoners under control; very little is actually spent on trying to correct or rehabilitate offenders.

Probation services should include securing meaningful employment and assisting probationers to retain their jobs by teaching them better work habits and providing vocational training. Finding probationers and their families decent housing and providing guidance counseling, as well as a variety of other services, should be integral parts of probation programs. In times of economic stress the argument is advanced that this reform is unrealistic, since many law-abiding citizens cannot secure jobs and decent housing. The argument begs the question, however, for these services should of course be made available to all citizens who require them.

Probation officers must be given smaller caseloads, must be more carefully selected and must be better trained and supervised. Even the present standards we hope to achieve fall far short of meaningful rehabilitation for offenders. A model of fifty cases per probation worker has been proposed. But how much time does that leave for the help which must be provided to each probationer? It is more likely that several hours a week of supervision, meetings, and arranging for the needs of offenders is a more realistic prescription for a successful rehabilitation program. It may be necessary to assign only ten or twenty probationers to every probation officer. This will result in a cost of approximately one thousand dollars or less per offender—a low price to pay for a reduced recidivism rate. It costs several thousand dollars each year to keep offenders in prison, and when they commit additional crimes additional expenses are incurred to arrest, adjudicate and perhaps incarcerate them all over again.

In virtually all large cities, and in some medium- and small-size cities, full-time probation staffs are attached to lower criminal courts. They supervise misdemeanants placed on probation—which in some cities may mean as little as a requirement of a monthly form letter from probationers. They also provide investigative services in connection with the sentencing function, inquiring into the backgrounds of potential probationers so that intelligent decisions can be made by the court. In some smaller cities there may be a part-time staff of one or two probation officers assigned to the lower court; in other cities there are none.

In 1960 an innovative probation program was begun in Royal Oak, Michigan, a suburb of Detroit, which has since been adopted in some form in more than one thousand lower criminal and juvenile courts. The program, now sponsored by an organization called Volunteers in Probation, Inc., is designed to compensate for the limited probation component available to the courts. Under professional supervision it draws upon volunteers, people in a variety of professions and business, to supervise and render assistance (and concern) to probationers placed in their custody. Professional counseling services are incorporated into the program for the type of supportive help which volunteers cannot provide. In some respects, the volunteers act as "big brothers," offering needed personal attention and serving as models for offenders—generally youths—entrusted to their care. Each volunteer has a caseload of one. The volunteers meet periodically with their probationers; they chat, go to ballgames together, discuss the probationers' problems and review the kind of adjustment being made to these problems. Volunteers encourage young people in their care to return to school and develop skills, and they help their charges find jobs.

As the program expanded to other communities, variations on the original Royal Oaks project were developed to suit local needs. The reports received have been for the most part extremely favorable. Reduced recidivism rates have attested to the value of using good and concerned people to provide assistance to youths in trouble.

The volunteer programs to date have been established in small and medium-size cities. Although there may be some reluctance in larger cities to establish a program seemingly tailored for smaller communities, the basic concept is adaptable to cities of all sizes. In larger cities there may be more need for a centralized and structured supervision of volunteers; perhaps an organization would be better suited to coordinate the volunteers so that defendants could be assigned directly to the organization. In such a program, reports would be submitted by the volunteers to the organization and a full record of meetings between defendants and volunteer helpers would be available for review by the courts.

The rationale for attempting a volunteer probation program in any city was provided by Joe Alex Morris in a few words in his recent book, *First Offender,*[20] about the Royal Oak experiment: ". . . intensive probation is one of the best weapons against crime and . . . it is possible in the lower courts only by the use of volunteers."

X YOUTH CRIME

Crime committed by youth is responsible for a good deal of the fear alluded to in Chapter I. Official statistics also reveal the extent of the serious crime problem attributable to young people. The National Crime Commission reported that for crimes of burglary, larceny and auto theft, "15-year-olds are arrested more often than persons of any other age, with 16-year-olds a close second." [1] In recent years more than sixty-five percent of all those arrested for forcible rape, eighty percent arrested for burglary, and nearly seventy percent arrested for robbery were under the age of twenty-five. Interestingly, the percentage of crimes committed by young people has increased substantially over the past few years. Even in the ten-to-fourteen age group, between 1958 and 1967 there was a three hundred percent increase in the incidence of conduct which would have constituted assault and robbery if engaged in by adults. In view of these statistics, the increasing proportion of young people in the general population (caused by the higher birth rates in post–World War II years) must be viewed as a related factor in the rising crime rates. There simply are more young people today than ever before, and the more there are the more crimes we are apt to have.

A sampling of probation reports in any criminal court will reveal that a large proportion of criminal offenders had juvenile-court records—some very long ones—for delinquency and related infractions. Their experience in juvenile courts should have been ample warning that they were engaged in transgressions that would have been criminal were they old enough to be charged with crimes. The tragic inability of juvenile courts to check the clearly indicated course of their wards' lives contributes enormously to the incidence of youthful and adult criminality in this country. No discussion of the criminal-justice system can be complete without consideration of the ever-mounting flood of graduates from juvenile courts into the criminal courts.

The importance of considering the specific problem of youth crime and the solutions which must be sought were expressed by the National Crime Commission: "It is simply more critical that young people be kept from crime, for they are the Nation's future, and their conduct will affect society for a long time to come. They are not yet set in their ways; they are still developing . . ."[2]

At the turn of the century it was felt that youthful deviancy was the beginning of criminality—that truancy, incorrigibility and other rebellious conduct were a sign of future trouble—but children were regarded as inherently salvageable, and so a separate body of laws and a separate court procedure were established. Curbing delinquency in its incipiency was the theme of this early reform movement. The juvenile-court system was the result of a desire for separate handling of children, with emphasis on rehabilitation.

Since the avowed purpose of court proceedings was not to punish children but to help them, a minimum of stress was placed on the rights of the accused. Even in recent years, when safeguards have been expanded in juvenile courts, there is a prevailing philosophy that these courts should be primarily concerned with the child, his protection and his benefit. This philosophy, of course, is often at odds with that of a vocal public demanding greater protection from the criminal acts of juveniles. The very terminology of the juvenile courts reflects the attempt to maintain their early goals.

The child brought to court today is charged with juvenile delinquency, not a crime; he is a "respondent," not a defendant; he answers to a "petition," not a complaint or an indictment; he "admits" or "denies" the allegations, he does not plead guilty or not guilty; he may be "adjudicated," never convicted; he may be "placed" in a "training school," never sentenced to a prison, jail or penitentiary.

Since it was deviancy, and not necessarily technically criminal conduct, that was regarded as the danger signal, juvenile-delinquency laws were directed at a wide range of youthful incorrigibility. The jurisdiction of the courts was invoked when the child appeared to need supervision; in fact, the label "In need of supervision" is commonly used today to bring into court children who have not committed what is regarded as a criminal act. One study revealed that nearly half of all children's cases brought into juvenile courts involved behavior which could not be defined as criminal under laws applicable to adults.

Essentially, there are two types of courts which regularly deal with youth crime. The first is the juvenile court (known in some jurisdictions as a children's court or family court). The second is the ordinary criminal court. The jurisdiction of juvenile courts is limited by specific maximum-age criteria (established by law) which vary to some degree from state to state. In approximately two thirds of the states, youths under the age of eighteen are subject to the jurisdiction of a juvenile court. In other states the maximum age is sixteen. All youths above a certain age are subject to the jurisdiction of adult courts. In most states there is some provision for transferring children's cases to adult courts when it is deemed warranted.

Not all violations of law by youths or children result in referral to juvenile court. As indicated in Chapter V (dealing with the diversion of individual defendants to other programs), it is often the practice not to proceed against children even when the allegations of unlawful behavior can be substantiated. The police in the exercise of their discretion do not refer all instances of delinquency to court. And some form of intake service often screens cases in court, culling out those which seem not to require court handling. It is believed that at least half and possibly up to three quarters of all cases which could be brought to juvenile court are screened out by the police outside the courthouse and by intake services in the courthouse.

The broad discretion given to police in determining which cases to handle informally has encouraged social scientists to examine the criteria upon which these decisions are based. Some studies have found that the demeanor, grooming, dress and race of juveniles were important variables in determining which cases would be sent to court. Juveniles who fit the popular physical stereotypes of delinquents were found to be stopped more frequently on the streets and treated more severely by the police. Disrespect for the police, according to the results of these studies, is a major factor in the police decision to invoke the court process.

The screening performed by intake procedures in juvenile courts was criticized by the National Crime Commission for being "an end in itself," since only rarely is an attempt made as part of this intake process to provide services to those screened out of the courts. Other criticism by the Crime Commission was directed at the practice of forcing children, as a condition for being screened out, to perform certain chores or to enter and remain in places of detention.

The juvenile-court movement contemplated a procedure of informal hearings without counsel and with heavy reliance upon a probation staff as directed by the judge to achieve the desired goals. Many of the juvenile-court laws simply provided that the hearings should be conducted in an "informal manner," without any indication of the degree of informality intended. Strict rules of evidence, however, were expressly waived. The strict burden of proof placed on prosecutors in criminal cases was not imposed. As late as 1967 the Crime Commission found that representation by counsel was not a regular feature of juvenile-court proceedings. Contrary to the practice of the criminal courts, the background data on the juvenile were considered relevant in the juvenile-court judge's determination.

The Crime Commission concluded that "the great hopes originally held for the juvenile court have not been fulfilled." [3] The courts have not been given the professional assistance needed to perform their functions. Low salaries and large caseloads make it difficult to render assistance to the youngsters brought into court. A 1963 survey, relied upon by the Commission, revealed a shocking scarcity of psychological and psychiatric services as well as other auxiliary services. The relatively few clinics which exist have long waiting lists and provide minimal treatment. "One reason for the failure of the juvenile courts," said the Crime Commission, "has been the community's continuing unwillingness to provide the resources—the people and facilities and concern—necessary to permit them to realize their potential and prevent them from taking on some of the undesirable features typical of lower criminal courts in this country." [4]

The Commission observed that the dispositional alternatives, following adjudication of delinquency or need of supervision, even in the better-endowed juvenile courts, do not measure up to the aspirations of the founders of the juvenile-court process. Generally there are three alternatives: outright release, probation and institutionalization. The first two provide no meaningful supervision. Institutionalization, according to the Commission, means storage "in an overcrowded, understaffed, high-security institution with little education, little vocational training, little counseling or job placement or other guidance upon release." [5] A 1966 report of a comprehensive study of institutions for juveniles, rendered by the National Council on Crime and Delinquency, drew these conclusions as to juvenile (pre-hearing) detention: that ninety-three percent of the country's juvenile-court jurisdictions (in which forty-four percent of the population lives) "have no place of detention other than a county jail or public lockup," that "children under seven years of age have been held in substandard county jails for lack of shelter care in foster homes," and that less than half of the nation's juvenile-detention homes (in the seven percent of the jurisdictions which have them) have provision for recreational facilities. Probation services for juveniles, the study found, are not available to many children who need them, and where such services are available they "may be given by staff carrying such enormous caseloads that any expectations of meaningful service are unrealistic." As for juvenile aftercare (following release from an institution), that was described as "a monument to neglect."

A review of juvenile detention in New York City portrays some of the serious problems created by underfinanced detention facilities. In March 1967 a state legislative committee held public hearings on the status of juvenile detention centers in New York City. Witnesses testified that the facilities were run like a concentration camp, that medical care was unavailable, and that self-induced abortions, brutality, and homosexuality were common. A grand jury, following an eight-month investigation, charged that brutality, aggressive homosexuality, overcrowding and poor medical care were all prevalent. The grand jury urged that there be improved medical, psychiatric and rehabilitative services and facilities, that children be grouped by age and offense, and that there be a maximum of fifteen children in each dormitory.

The management and control of New York City's detention facilities were transferred to the Office of Probation, subject to supervision by the Appellate Divisions of the State Supreme Court. Those courts appointed a three-member panel to investigate conditions at the juvenile detention facilities. The panel found that "many children who did not require secure detention were being detained in the completely-locked, prison-like, maximum-security" detention facilities. The cost of maintaining a child in these facilities was placed at fifteen thousand dollars a year! The facilities were described as "depressing," as having "wet and falling plaster," as needing painting and better lighting. The gymnasium is one of the buildings was described as a "medium-sized, dilapidated room with two large poles in the center which restrict any mobile activity." Recreational programs were found to be "woefully inadequate." The panel urged the replacement of two of three buildings used to detain juveniles. "Both of these facilities," said the panel, "are in such deplorable condition as to constitute a serious danger and hazard to the health and safety of occupants." Homosexuality, both consensual and nonconsensual, physical attacks (by children on one another and on staff, and by staff on children), and drug use within the institutions were all noted as problems requiring attention. It was urged that the use of solitary confinement in an empty room be discontinued and that a range of administrative reforms be instituted.

Both the National Crime Commission and the United States Supreme Court have been critical of the lack of due-process safeguards, which are so important a part of court proceedings. Representation by counsel, we have seen, often was not a part of the proceedings. Specific charges often were not drawn or, if drawn, were not served on the accused or his parents. The informality of proceedings resulted in ten- to fifteen-minute hearings, during which the accusing witnesses were seldom cross-examined and the accused generally was expected to be a witness against himself. Incarceration at times was for periods longer than adults could have received for the same unlawful conduct. In the 1967 Gault case,[6] in which the Supreme Court ordered new procedural safeguards for juveniles, the accused had been committed by an Arizona juvenile court to custody for a maximum period of six years. If he had been eighteen at the time he committed the offense (of making offensive telephone calls) the maximum punishment would have been two months imprisonment and a fifty-dollar fine.

The United States Supreme Court decision in the Gault case had a substantial impact on proceedings in most juvenile courts. The court held, first, that notice of the charges lodged must be given to the child in advance of scheduled court proceedings, to allow time for preparation of a defense, and that the charges were to set forth the specific alleged misconduct. Second, a child accused of serious misconduct has the right to counsel—to retain his own lawyer if he is able to afford one or, if he is not, to be given the free services of counsel. Third, every child accused of juvenile delinquency has a right to have his accusers cross-examined by counsel and cannot be compelled, consistent with the Constitution, to testify at any phase of the court proceeding.

The Crime Commission, in the same critical vein as the courts, found that present screening measures used to determine which accused juveniles will not be brought before the courts are inadequate. It noted that in some cases juveniles who required court adjudication and social-service care were being screened out; in other cases, juveniles who qualified for less stringent handling were held for adjudication. The Commission recommended an expanded use of community agencies for dealing with delinquents—as an alternative, in many cases, to prosecution for juvenile delinquency. A youth services bureau was urged as the vehicle for such alternative dispositions. A bureau of this sort would pull together all of the community resources and make an appropriate referral in each case.

The question of the juvenile court's jurisdiction over conduct not regarded as criminal if committed by adults was also discussed by the Commission. Reference was made to a law which establishes a category labeled "in need of supervision" for those whose general incorrigibility does not equal adult criminal behavior or who are victims of parental neglect or other circumstances against which they need protection. The Commission observed that the new label also has the tendency to impose a stigma on children who are adjudicated in this manner. Without opposing this lesser form of delinquency, the Commission recommended that in such cases greater use of alternatives be pursued before there is recourse to the courts.

Every effort should be made, as urged by the Crime Commission, to marshal community resources and use them as an alternative to court processing. But in appropriate cases the courts should strive to interrupt patterns of juvenile conduct which seem headed for a life of crime. The courts should be aware, of course, of ill-considered or inefficient official intervention which only increases the chances of children's becoming adult criminals. Sending children to overcrowded, regimented and underfinanced juvenile institutions probably does more to aggravate than alleviate the delinquency problem. These institutions, often called training schools, become schools for crime. Children are thrown together with their peers and, at times, with adult offenders, and they teach one another new methods of "making it" (the easy way). Often they become hardened by these experiences and graduate to more serious crime.

As in the case of the adult offender, and perhaps of more importance here, the stress should be on community corrections. More resources must be made available. More skills, more time, more facilities, more training, more attention to the needs of youths in trouble are necessary elements of proper handling by the courts. Without these the courts will fail, as they have in the past.

A study of ten thousand young offenders in Philadelphia is revealing. Six percent of these boys (427 of them) accounted for most of the arrests compiled by all of them for homicide, rape and assault. These 427, by official statistics, committed seventy-one percent of the robberies.[7] This suggests that a large proportion of violent crimes is being committed by repeaters, many of whom have actually been identified as delinquent early in their careers. If the court and a sound correctional process can do something with a proven delinquent at an early stage, future misery, hardship and crime may well be averted.

EPILOGUE

In his address to the National Conference on the Judiciary on March 11, 1971, President Nixon stressed delay as the major problem facing the overloaded courts of America:

> The law's delay creates bail problems, as well as overcrowded jails; it forces judges to accept pleas of guilty to lesser offenses just to process the caseload—to "give away the courthouse for the sake of the calendar." Without proper safeguards, this can turn a court of justice into a mill of injustice.

Delay works to the disadvantage of the innocent defendant as well as the prosecution. There are certain consequences of delay in reaching trial that can be disastrous to both—such as disappearance of witnesses, difficulty in preserving evidence and dimming of memories of events. Aside from the ultimate result, the waiting period before disposition can be a searing, ruinous experience for a defendant. All defendants incarcerated pending trial should be brought to trial as soon as possible.

But prompt disposition of criminal cases is only part of the answer. At every stage of the criminal-justice process—arrest, in some cases the period before arrest, in court, probation, correction—there must be intelligent and considerate treatment. Justice must be administered patiently and thoughtfully; instant justice can be mischievous.

Whatever recommendations I have made for removing certain categories of crimes from the criminal-justice system or increasing its resources and operating efficiency are not merely to churn out more dispositions. Hopefully, if these measures are adopted, sufficient time and means will be afforded to treat with dignity and fairness every person caught up in the criminal-justice processes; punishment or efforts to rehabilitate and reclaim would follow.

In a short article on the Attica uprising in the New York *Times* of September 29, 1971, Herbert Sturz, director of the Vera Institute of Justice, wrote movingly and compellingly on what must be done to avert future outbreaks. Sturz eloquently demonstrates the essential elements of understanding and compassion that must be provided all along the road to Attica and the interdependence of the various agencies functioning on that road:

> Imagine Attica rebuilt—black and Spanish-speaking guards, better food, censorship eased, the screens between visitors and inmates removed, full freedom of religion, daily showers available. There are classrooms, counseling sessions and access to a good library. Officials are making an effort to remember that inmates are human beings.
>
> In spite of such good deeds, good intentions, and money spent, it is clear that those sentenced to the new Attica will arrive with the stamp of the ghetto and the scars of detention pens upon them. They will arrive at Attica hurt and angry and brutalized. The new and improved Attica will, of course, still take away their freedom, and produce resentful, bitter, even vengeful men.
>
> Rebuild Attica? Yes. Make it more humane, of course. But let's not deceive ourselves, Attica reformed will not correct, nor will it rehabilitate. What it will do is provide society with temporary protection from those who have been identified as threatening.
>
> But we can do more than contain people. We can in fact rehabilitate—and thus provide not only genuine protection for society, but some chance for productive lives. But to rehabilitate we must intervene at every way station on the road to Attica.

The road to Attica begins with families uprooted, with bad housing, racial prejudices, drug profiteering; with schools and social agencies unresponsive; with kids growing up feeling left out. Improving the quality of life for these persons would result in fewer setting foot in jail or prison.

Meanwhile, we must bring about changes where we can. Arrest is the earliest time for society to intervene. Every effort should be made to keep an accused person out of jail, where he can only become angrier and more bitter. Whenever possible a summons should be issued by the police in lieu of a formal arrest.

Pretrial service agencies staffed by community liaison specialists should divert the accused into the custody of a community agency. That agency would see that the person comes to court when required and try to help him find a job, deal with his drug habit, or obtain more education.

Intervention after arrest can often circumvent the need for prosecution. The Court Employment Project, begun as a small pilot experiment in Manhattan four years ago, gets jobs and provides counseling, group therapy, and a structured program to persons awaiting trial. If participants get and hold a job and remain crime-free for three months, charges are dismissed by the court. . . .

Less than half a cent of every criminal-justice dollar goes to rehabilitation. That half doesn't go far.

Many men now in Attica should be pre-released to a structured work environment in the community like that provided by Pioneer Services in New York City, a corporation which hires a man only if he has a criminal record, a history of drug abuse or alcoholism, and has been unable to hold a job anywhere else. . . .

Those who have taken the road to Attica can come back if we give them the resources and the opportunity.

NOTES

INTRODUCTION

1. Philip Ennis, *Criminal Victimization in the United States: A Report of a National Survey*, Field Survey II, President's Commission on Law Enforcement and the Administration of Justice (Washington: U.S. Govt. Printing Office, 1967).
2. *International Herald Tribune*, Aug. 26, 1971.
3. *The Challenge of Crime in a Free Society*, Report by the President's Commission on Law Enforcement and the Administration of Justice (Washington: U.S. Govt. Printing Office, 1967), p. 279.

CHAPTER I

1. *Criminal Justice Plan for 1971*, Report of the New York City Criminal Justice Coordinating Council, p. 6.
2. *Newsweek*, March 8, 1971, p. 23.
3. New York *Times*, June 27, 1971, Sect. 4, p. 16.
4. The *Reporter Dispatch*, White Plains, N.Y., Nov. 12, 1968, p. 14.
5. New York *Times*, July 29, 1966, p. 27.

CHAPTER II

1. *Prisons, Probation and Parole in the District of Columbia*, Report by the Committee on Prisons, Probation and Parole of the Board of Commissioners of the District of Columbia (unpublished, April 1957), pp. 113-19.
2. Thomas F. A. Plaut, *Alcohol Problems, A Report to the Nation*, Cooperative Commission on the Study of Alcoholism (New York: Oxford Univ. Press, 1967), p. 61.
3. *Drunkenness*, Task Force Report, President's Commission on Law Enforcement and the Administration of Justice (Washington:

U.S. Govt. Printing Office, 1967), p. 2.
4. Francis A. Allen, "The Borderland of the Criminal Law: Problems of 'Socializing' Criminal Justice," *The Social Service Review*, Vol. 32, June 1958, p. 109.
5. Driver v. Hinnant, 356 F.2d 761 (4th Cir. 1966); Easter v. District of Columbia, 361 F.2d 50 (D.C. Cir. 1966).
6. Driver v. Hinnant, *supra*, note 5.
7. Robinson v. California, 370 U.S. 660 (1962).
8. Powell v. Texas, 392 U.S. 514 (1968).
9. *Ibid.* at 528.
10. *Report of the President's Commission on Crime in the District of Columbia* (Washington: U.S. Govt. Printing Office, 1966), p. 485.
11. New York *Times,* Dec. 14, 1967, p. 52.
12. Richard H. Blum, "Mind-Altering Drugs and Dangerous Behavior: Alcohol," in *Drunkenness,* Task Force Report, President's Commission on Law Enforcement and the Administration of Justice (Washington: U.S. Govt. Printing Office, 1967), Appendix B, p. 40.
13. New York *Times,* Sept. 10, 1971, p. 37.
14. Mapp v. Ohio, 367 U.S. 643 (1961).
15. People v. Berrios, 28 N.Y.2d 361, 370 (Dissent of Chief Judge Fuld) (1971).
16. Robinson v. California, 370 U.S. 660 (1962).
17. Transcripts of proceedings, District of Columbia v. Boyd, D.C. Ct. of Gen. Sess., No. DC-16, 852-66 p. 24 (June 21, 1966).
18. New York *Times,* April 21, 1969, pp. 1, 42.
19. *Ibid.*
20. Powell v. Texas, 392 U.S. 514, 529 (1968).
21. *Yale Law Journal,* Vol. 78 (1969), p. 1175; Herman Joseph and Vincent P. Dole, "Methadone Patients on Probation and Parole," *Federal Probation,* Vol. 34, June 1970, p. 42.
22. Carl Chambers, *The Incidence and Patterns of Drug Abuse among Long-Term Methadone Maintenance Patients,* New York State Narcotics Addiction Control Commission (unpublished, 1971), p. 4.

CHAPTER III

1. Leonard Scandur, "Cash Register Justice," *The Nation,* Vol. 198, Feb. 10, 1964, p. 144.
2. New York *Times,* June 15, 1971, p. 17.

CHAPTER IV

1. Herbert Packer, *The Limits of the Criminal Sanction* (Stanford, Calif.: Stanford Univ. Press, 1968), pp. 259-60.

2. New York *Times,* July 24, 1969, p. 34.
3. State v. Clark, 58 N.J. 2d 72, 275 A.2d 137 (Sup. Ct. 1971).
4. New York *Times,* Feb. 14, 1971, p. 40.
5. News release, New York City Health Services Administration, June 29, 1971.
6. *Organized Crime,* Task Force Report, President's Commission on Law Enforcement and the Administration of Justice (Washington: U.S. Govt. Printing Office, 1967), p. 3.
7. New York *Times,* Sept. 13, 1971, p. 1.
8. *Ibid.,* Sept. 22, 1971, p. 94.
9. *New York Law Journal,* Vol. 163, No. 2 (Feb. 20, 1970), pp. 1, 3.
10. *The Report of the Commission on Obscenity and Pornography* (Washington: U.S. Govt. Printing Office, September 1970), p. 52.
11. *An Assessment of Drug Use in the General Population,* New York State Narcotics Addiction Control Commission (May 1971), p. 96.
12. *Life,* Oct. 31, 1969, p. 34.

CHAPTER VI

1. Baldwin v. New York, 399 U.S. 66 (1970).
2. Miranda v. Arizona, 384 U.S. 436, 448 (1966).
3. *See* Miranda v. Arizona, 384 U.S. 436, 452 (1966).
4. *See* Miranda v. Arizona, 384 U.S. 436, 453 (1966).
5. *See* Miranda v. Arizona, 384 U.S. 436, 449 (1966).
6. *Ibid.*
7. Miranda v. Arizona, 384 U.S. 436 (1966).
8. Mapp v. Ohio, 367 U.S. 643 (1961).
9. Lankford v. Gelston, 364 F.2d 197 (1966).
10. New York *Post,* March 16, 1971, p. 2.

CHAPTER VII

1. The *Reporter Dispatch,* June 23, 1971, p. 47.
2. New York *Times,* July 10, 1971, p. 9.
3. New York: Atheneum, 1967, pp. 73-78.
4. *New York Law Journal,* Vol. 165, No. 107 (June 4, 1971), p. 1.
5. Benanti v. United States, 355 U.S. 96 (1957).
6. Edward Bennett Williams, "The Wiretapping-Eavesdropping Problem: A Defense Counsel's View," *Minnesota Law Review,* Vol. 44 (1960), pp. 855, 858.
7. *Report of the President's Commission on Crime in the District of Columbia* (Washington: U.S. Govt. Printing Office, 1966), p. 198.
8. Analysis of published reports

of the Law Enforcement Assistance Program.
9. Analysis of *First Annual Report of the Law Enforcement Assistance Administration* (Washington: U.S. Govt. Printing Office, 1969).
10. *Law and Disorder II, State Planning and Programming under Title I of the Omnibus Crime Control and Safe Streets Act of 1968.* Prepared by the National Urban Coalition, Vol. II, p. 5.
11. New York *Times,* June 13, 1971, p. 83.
12. Bruce J. Terris, "The Role of the Police," *Annals of the American Academy of Political and Social Science,* Vol. 374, November 1967, pp. 58, 65.
13. *Ibid.,* pp. 65-66.
14. *Ibid.,* p. 66; Field Survey III, *Studies in Crime and Law Enforcement in Major Metropolitan Areas,* Report of a research study submitted to the President's Commission on Law Enforcement and the Administration of Justice (Washington: U. S. Govt. Printing Office, 1966), Vol. II, Sect. 1, p. 135.
15. New York *Times,* Nov. 29, 1970, p. 32.
16. *The Police,* Task Force Report, President's Commission on Law Enforcement and the Administration of Justice (Washington: U.S. Govt. Printing Office, 1967), Ch. 7, p. 208.
17. New York *Times,* July 5, 1968, p. 1.
18. *New York Law Journal,* Vol. 166, No. 2 (July 2, 1971), p. 1.

CHAPTER VIII

1. *Report of the National Advisory Commission on Civil Disorders* (New York: Bantam Books, 1968); Comments, *Michigan Law Review,* Vol. 66 (1968), p. 1542; see Botein and Stern, "Civil Liberties and Civil Disorders: Are They Reconcilable?," *New York Law Forum,* Winter 1968, p. 763.
2. Report of the Baltimore Committee on the Administration of Justice under Emergency Conditions (unpublished, May 31, 1968).
3. *The Challenge of Crime in a Free Society,* Report of the President's Commission on Law Enforcement and the Administration of Justice (Washington: U.S. Govt. Printing Office, 1967), p. 128.
4. *The Forgotten Army,* Report by the Committee on Criminal Courts of the Charity Organization Society of the City of New York (1911–1917).
5. Richard W. Velde, *The Correctional Trainer,* Newsletter for the Illinois Correctional Staff, Fall 1970, p. 109, cited in Richard A. McGee, "Our Sick Jails," *Federal Probation,* Vol. 35, No. 1 (March 1971), p. 3.
6. New York *Times,* Jan. 7, 1971, p. 1.
7. *Ibid.,* Dec. 12, 1966, p. 1.

8. *Ibid.*, June 25, 1969, p. 94; March 31, 1970, p. 29; May 24, 1970, p. 56; Sept. 17, 1970, p. 42.
9. *Ibid.*, March 5, 1971, p. 32.
10. Washington *Post,* Sept. 9, 1966, p. A-3.
11. *Ibid.*, June 23, 1966, p. A-1.
12. New York *Times,* Oct. 13, 1967, p. 29.
13. *Ibid.*, Aug. 22, 1970, p. 22.
14. New York *Post,* April 9, 1969, p. 30.
15. James V. Bennett, "Of Prisons and Justice" (1961), in *A Selection of Writings of James V. Bennett,* prepared for the Subcommittee on National Penitentiaries of the Committee on the Judiciary, U.S. Senate, April 16, 1964, pp. 317, 320.
16. Seminar and Institute on the Disparity of Sentences for the Sixth, Seventh and Eighth Judicial Circuits, under the auspices of the Judicial Conference of the United States, Highland Park, Ill., Oct. 12 and 13, 1961, 30 Fed. Rules Decisions 401, in Report of Hearing before the Subcommittee on National Penitentiaries of the Committee on the Judiciary, U.S. Senate, Jan. 22, 1964, pp. 281, 285, Table 5A.
17. New York *Times,* Jan. 28, 1968, p. 76.

CHAPTER IX

1. *Corrections in the United States.* National Council on Crime and Delinquency (1966).
2. Elmer K. Nelson Jr., "Community Board Correctional Treatment," *Annals of the American Academy of Political and Social Science,* Vol. 374, November 1967, p. 82.
3. *Corrections in the United States, supra,* note 1, at 155.
4. *Report of President's Commission on Crime in the District of Columbia* (Washington: U.S. Govt. Printing Office, 1966), p. 435.
5. The *Reporter Dispatch,* Jan. 20, 1971, p. 9.
6. Bruce R. Jacob, "Prison Discipline and Inmates' Rights" *Harvard Civil Liberties Law Review,* Vol. V, April 1970, pp. 227, 235-40.
7. *Ibid.*, p. 237.
8. New York *Times,* Sept. 3, 1970, p. 45.
9. *Corrections,* Task Force Report, President's Commission on Law Enforcement and the Administration of Justice (Washington: U.S. Govt. Printing Office, 1967), p. 46.
10. New York *Times,* Feb. 2, 1971, p. 62; letter from Dr. Frank L. Rundle dated April 26, 1971.
11. The *Reporter Dispatch,* July 9, 1971, p. 40.
12. *Ibid.*, June 16, 1971, p. 11.
13. John P. Conrad, *Crime and Its Correction* (Berkeley: Univ. of California Press, 1967).
14. *Ibid.*, p. 131.
15. Norval Morris, "Lessons from the Adult Correctional System of

Sweden," *Federal Probation,* Vol. 30, No. 4 (December 1966), p. 3.
16. See John D. Case, "Doing Time in the Community," *Federal Probation,* Vol. 31, No. 1 (March 1967), p. 9; Elmer F. Anderson, "Work Release Sentencing," *ibid.,* Vol. 28, No. 4 (December 1964), p. 7.
17. *Fortune News,* November 1970.
18. *Corrections in the United States, supra,* note 1, at 169.
19. Nelson, *supra,* note 2, at 84.
20. New York: Funk and Wagnalls, 1970.

CHAPTER X

1. *The Challenge of Crime in a Free Society,* Report of the President's Commission on Law Enforcement and the Administration of Justice (Washington: U.S. Govt. Printing Office, 1967), p. 44.
2. *Ibid.,* p. 58.
3. *Juvenile Delinquency and Youth Crime,* Task Force Report, President's Commission on Law Enforcement and the Administration of Justice (Washington: U.S. Govt. Printing Office, 1967), p. 7.
4. *Ibid.*
5. *Ibid.,* p. 8.
6. *In re* Gault, 387 U.S. 1 (1967).
7. *To Establish Justice, To Ensure Domestic Tranquility,* Report of the National Commission on the Causes and Prevention of Violence (New York: Award Books, 1969), pp. 24, 28.

INDEX